Familiar Spirits

By Robert D. Shackelford

©Promised Land Publications
Robert Shackelford Publishing

Scripture References are from The New American
Standard and The King James translations of the Bible.
All emphasis on Scripture is the Author's.

A FEW WORDS ABOUT THIS BOOK BY:
CHARLES AND FRANCES HUNTER

FAMILIAR SPIRITS is a much needed book. Too many Christians do not understand the power and the operation of demonic spirits.

Robert Shackelford has written a book which will open the eyes of the believer who wants to understand more about the tactics of the devil and how to conquer over them.

Many people will have questions answered for them in the chapter "Can The Devil Read Your Mind?"

If the book had just told about Familiar Spirits, it would not accomplish a lot, but it tells you how to confuse the Familiar Spirits so that you will come out the winner.

A fascinating book with a great potential! We would recommend a study of this book by all those who are hungry to know how to stomp on the devil.

Charles and Frances Hunter
Hunter Ministries

A FEW MORE WORDS ABOUT THIS BOOK BY:
GERALD DERSTINE.

Being personally acquainted with the author, Robert Shackelford, for many years, I know this book, "FAMILIAR SPIRITS", is written from a vast bastion of knowledge, experience and wisdom. We need to know how the wiles of the flesh influence our Christian walk.

This book will be a great help to you in discerning the enemy who so cleverly attacks us and attempts to keep us in ignorance. We need to become wiser to enable us to deal with the tactics of Satan.

Let this book instruct you and reveal the God-given rights you have in Jesus Christ. After you have read it, share the contents with your other Christian friends.

Gerald Derstine, D.D.
President, Gospel Crusade, Inc.
Christian Retreat
Bradenton, Florida

PREFACE

I started this study on "FAMILIAR SPIRITS" when I began to experience and to see the damage the enemy was and is almost constantly inflicting on the Body of Christ. The Bible tells us that we are in a War - And that the Weapons of our Warfare are not of the flesh, but divinely powerful for the destruction of fortresses. Beloved, until we realize these basic facts, we will lose many battles to the enemy.

This book is dedicated to all those who are tired of losing battles! To every Believer who wants to destroy the strongholds the devil has built and fortified in their lives and in the lives of their loved ones.

Robert D. Shackelford

CONTENTS

INTRODUCTION

YOUR ADVERSARY

Peter, by the inspiration of the Holy Spirit, instructs us in 1 Peter 5:8:

"BE OF SOBER SPIRIT, BE ON THE ALERT. YOUR ADVERSARY, THE DEVIL, PROWLS ABOUT LIKE A ROARING LION, SEEKING SOMEONE TO DEVOUR."

Have you been hearing any strange noises in your ears lately? Has the devil been roaring around in your life?

The Holy Spirit told Peter to tell you that someone is trying to devour you! Then He identifies the one who is trying to devour you as your adversary; and then He specifically tells you that your adversary is the devil.

Does it come as a shock to some of you wives that your adversary is not your husband? Men, the one seeking to devour you is not that sweet thing you promised the moon to - it is not your boss, or your neighbors; or your parents; it isn't even your children!

The one who is trying to devour you is the devil, the accuser of the brethren!

Have you ever thought that the devil might have you on his menu? How are you listed do you suppose - as a snack? A full course dinner? Brunch maybe? An after the meeting dessert?

Maybe it is your peace that he is trying to devour, or your marriage, or your career. It might even be your health, or your adequacy. We do know for certain that the devil is your adversary, and that he is trying to devour you - because that is what the Bible says, and we know that The Word of God is the truth!

"...BE ON THE ALERT...YOUR ADVERSARY, THE DEVIL IS SEEKING SOMEONE TO DEVOUR!"

Do you want to see how your adversary operates? Let's take a look at Job 1:6-7:

"NOW THERE WAS A DAY WHEN THE SONS OF GOD CAME TO PRESENT THEMSELVES BEFORE THE LORD, AND SATAN CAME ALSO AMONG THEM. AND THE LORD SAID UNTO SATAN, 'WHENCE COMEST THOU?' THEN SATAN ANSWERED THE LORD AND SAID, 'FROM GOING TO AND FRO IN THE EARTH, AND FROM WALKING UP AND DOWN IN IT.' "

He might have said,

"I have been prowling around in Delaware, or in Los Angeles, or in Tulsa, or in the town where you live, seeking someone to devour."

"I have been looking for a chink in some- one's armor. I have been looking for a place where I can get a foothold. I have been searching for

an unprotected heart where I can stick one of my fiery darts."

"I have been pacing to and fro examining the menu! I have been window shopping! I stopped by the cafeteria to look at the entreès to decide who I am going to try to devour!"

Get this truth settled - You have an adversary! And Peter specifically identified your adversary as the Devil. Someone is going to try to mess up your life. If you never know the truth, and apply the truth to your life - you can never live in the fullness of the freedom that Christ purchased for you at Calvary.

Have you ever had any first-hand experience with your adversary? Has he been prowling down your street - trampling on your lawn - jumping on the flower bed of your life? Has he been stomping on your porch - has he been shaking your windows and rattling your doors?

I think that may be where the term "Shake, rattle, and roll" could have originated. Some Believer was in a battle with the devil, and the devil was doing his best to,

Shake him up - To rattle his faith in the Lord - And to roll him over to devour him! It does seem like that sometimes, doesn't it? - When everything appears to be going wrong, when your senses are rattling, when your body is rocking, and when your finances are getting a little shaky.

Listen to me now, when these things start happening in your life, you need to realize that

they are happening because your adversary is
trying to chomp on you!

One of the purposes of this book is to make you
inedible - to make you unappetizing - indigestible! To
make you so tough that you will give heartburn to the
guy who takes such delight in trying to take a bite out
of you.

Who is your adversary anyway? Who is the one
who is trying to do you in?

The word "satan" in Greek means "the accuser."
The word "devil" in Greek means "false accuser,
slanderer." The devil is your adversary, he is your
opponent. He is the one who accuses you and
slanders you to you and to your brethren.

Jesus also identified him as a liar and the father of
all lies in John 8:44, and then Jesus more fully
described the devil's objectives in John 10:10 when He
told us,

"THE THIEF COMES ONLY TO STEAL, TO KILL, AND TO DESTROY..."

I know that you must realize by now that the devil
did not come to give you life and life more abundantly!
Jesus said he came to steal from you! He came to kill
you! He came to destroy you! The devil is determined
to do you in!

You know now by definition and by your own
personal experience that the devil is the bad guy. Let's
look at how he operates.

He will oppose you! He will try to steal from
you, he will try to kill you, and he will try to

destroy you. He will try to keep you from getting and enjoying any good thing in life.

He will try to steal your health, your peace, your happiness, your career, your marriage, your integrity, your adequacy!

He will try to steal anything and everything good that he can take from you!

Jesus said the devil is a thief, and thieves thief! They steal! The devil will thief from you if you let him.

Aren't you grateful that the Bible teaches you how you can stop the thief from thiefing from you! Thank God the devil is not irresistible - he is resistible! You can resist the devil with the Word of God.

The Holy Spirit told James to tell us in James 4:7,

"SUBMIT THEREFORE TO GOD. RESIST THE DEVIL, AND HE WILL FLEE FROM YOU."

The Bible's instructions are very clear. First you submit to God, and then you resist the devil! Do you know that you always must do it in that order? It does not work any other way; you cannot resist the devil if you do not submit to God first! Are you listening?

Lots of folks have had some experience in resisting, but it seems as if most of the resisting they do is against the Word of God, and not against the devil.

They resist reading the Bible, they resist going to church; they resist studying to show

themselves approved. They resist tithing and
giving; they resist doing good! They resist
doing what God tells them to do in His Word.

Then they try to resist the devil, but it does not
work. Do you know why? They cannot resist the devil
because they have not followed God's devil resisting
instructions. Their wants and their desires are always
more important than God's wants and desires, and they
will not submit their lives to God. They are still doing
the things that seem best to them whether these things
agree with God's Word or not.

Listen to me carefully now, if you want Biblical
Results in your life, you must apply Biblical Principles!

That means that if you want what the Bible says in
your life, you must do what the Bible says! If you want
to be able to stop the Devourer from munching on you;
if you want to stop the roaring in your life; you must
submit to God.

Do you think it might be worth it?

Well of course it is. God gave us all the weapons
we need to defeat the devil in our lives, and now it is
time that we, as The Church of the Lord Jesus Christ,
began to use the weapons He provided.

The devil uses his weapons very effectively. And
he uses them every day - he uses anger, envy, strife,
jealousy, sickness, inadequacy - and all the other
weapons he has in his arsenal. And he always uses
them to his advantage.

Some of the spirits that our Adversary uses so
effectively against us are called "Familiar Spirits." The
purpose of this book is to expose them for what they
are, and to show you how you can defeat them in your
life.

SECTION 1

CHAPTER ONE
FAMILIAR SPIRITS

Isn't that an unusual title? The Holy Spirit certainly knows how to get our attention, doesn't He? He uses this term sixteen times in the King James translation of the Bible, and all of them, every single reference, is in the Old Testament. Since Familiar Spirits are only mentioned in the Old Testament, does that mean that they have been done away with? Have they ceased to exist? Have they become extinct like the pre-historic men some evolutionists like to reconstruct for us from a bone fragment or a tooth?

What are Familiar Spirits anyway? How do they act? What do they do? What does the Bible say about them? How do they get into your life, and when they get in - how do you get them out? How do you get rid of spirits?

These are some of the questions we will look at as we examine God's Word together for the answers on how to defeat the Spirits who have become familiar with you.

These spirits have one purpose. They have one goal in mind - and that goal is to defeat you!

*They are determined to keep you down! To walk
on you! To make you feel inadequate and
helpless, and unworthy and inferior. They bring
sickness, and unhappiness, and poverty, and
every other evil thing.*

Many times these spirits will operate in arrogance
through haughty know-it-all attitudes. They will try to
wreck your life! They will try to bring grief into your
life! Why some of these spirits have been hanging
around you for years, and you know they have not been
bringing you righteousness, and peace, and joy in the
Holy Ghost.

We will take a look at all of them, the short and the
tall, the big ones and the little ones, the spirits who flee
easily, as well as those who hang in there tenaciously.
We will look at the whole bunch, including the three
who have become familiar with almost every
household. I call them the three stooges: maybe you
have had some experience with them. I have named
them...

"DOUBT! DESPAIR! AND DOOM!"

Have these spirits been hanging around your
place? Have they become familiar with you?

How do the three stooges operate? How do they
manifest themselves? Well, their first objective is to try
to make you doubt the validity of God's Word. They
will try to bring doubt into your life:

*"O God is your Word really true? Can I really
believe for my household like Paul told the*

Philippian jailer in Acts 16:31? If I can, then why isn't my husband or my wife saved, because I have been praying for them for sixteen years or so?"

"What about adequacy, God? The Bible says I can do all things through Christ who strengthens me, but I do not feel like I can do lots of things. I know I am not strong! I just do not feel adequate!"

"What is the truth about healing, and peace, and all that prosperity stuff? Do all those good things belong to me in this life, or do I have to wait to enjoy the good in the life to come?"

"How about healing, God? Does Isaiah 53:5 actually mean what it says? Does it really, really mean that by His stripes I am healed? Is Isaiah talking about me? Does this Scripture include cancer and arthritis, or does it only apply to headaches and colds? Did healing pass away when the Apostles passed away? - Did healing pass away with John Wesley, or with Kathryn Kuhlman? Why do I still hurt after I have prayed?"

"Is your Word always the truth like Jesus said in John 17:17?"

Do you see how these spirits work?

They will try to bring doubt into your mind. Not doubt about the weather, or doubt about what you are going to wear tomorrow, or doubt about what time it is.

They will do their best to get you to doubt the validity of God's Word!

And as soon as a Doubtful spirit finds a little chink in your armor, he will begin to set up his camp in you. Then he will start building a fortified stronghold, and when he sees the walls of his stronghold beginning to rise in you, he will send out engraved invitations to his favorite friends, Despair and Doom!

And sure enough, as soon as you begin to doubt - Despair RSVPs and moves right on in, and Doom is on its way. It happens every time, these spirits never turn an invitation down!

When you begin to doubt the truthfulness of God's Word, Despair and Doom are just around the corner. You might as well save a place for them at your dinner table, and make up the guest bedroom, because you are going to have house guests - And this bunch will try to move in and live with you permanently! Listen to me now, when you doubt the validity of God's Word, you become an easy target for the three stooges.

Aren't you tired of these spirits?

Aren't you tired of them messing around in your life? Why some of these spirits run in and out of Believers' lives as if they had a key to their front doors.

Is that you? - Have you given them the master key to your life?

Have you installed a revolving door for them at your house? Do they come and go as they please?

Some of these spirits act as if they have your permission to build their kingdoms in your life, and when they start construction in you, they always bring a bunch of misery with them - Miserable misery spirits.

James warned us about the Spirit of Doubt in James 1:6-7:

"BUT LET HIM ASK IN FAITH WITHOUT
DOUBTING, FOR THE ONE WHO DOUBTS IS
LIKE THE SURF OF THE SEA DRIVEN AND
TOSSED BY THE WIND. FOR LET NOT THAT
MAN EXPECT THAT HE WILL RECEIVE
ANYTHING FROM THE LORD."

The one who doubts is a doubter - and you know
that doubter is not one of God's favorite titles, is it?
When you are presented to the Lord, when you enter
the Throne Room, and the trumpets blare, you do not
want the angel Gabriel to announce you with a shout
of "Here comes the doubter!" do you? Of course not!
You want to be presented as "A Believer," as one who
believes God's Word.

The spirits of Doubt and Unbelief will try to keep
you out of your Promised Land the same way they kept
the Children of Israel out of their Promised Land. That
is exactly what they did! The spirits of Doubt and
Unbelief kept the Children of Israel wandering around
in the wilderness all of their lives. Let's look at the
Biblical documentation of this statement.

Hebrews 3:18-19 states:

"AND TO WHOM DID HE (GOD) SWEAR THAT
THEY SHOULD NOT ENTER HIS REST, BUT
TO THOSE WHO WERE DISOBEDIENT? AND
SO WE SEE THAT THEY WERE NOT ABLE TO
ENTER BECAUSE OF UNBELIEF."

They could not enter the Promised Land because
of unbelief, and the situation has not changed. The
Bible says Jesus is still the same in Hebrews 13:8, and
you know by personal experience that the devil is still

the same. And the same old spirits of Doubt and Unbelief are still trying to do their thing in Believers' lives.

Their thing is to keep Believers out of the Promised Land!

Unfortunately these spirits have become familiar with so many Believers, that even though they are saved and some of them are full of God's Precious Spirit, they are still not living on the promises of God! Lots of Believers are still living on skimpy wilderness benefits. They have never realized or experienced the reality of Colossians 1:12-13 in their lives:

"GIVING THANKS TO THE FATHER, WHO HAS QUALIFIED US TO SHARE IN THE INHERITANCE OF THE SAINTS IN LIGHT. FOR HE DELIVERED US FROM THE DOMAIN OF DARKNESS, AND TRANSFERRED US TO THE KINGDOM OF HIS BELOVED SON."

The Kingdom of His Beloved Son is the Promised Land, isn't it? Sure it is! It is the place where all of the

"...PROMISES OF GOD ARE IN HIM, YEA AND IN HIM AMEN..."

All of the Promises of God are what? Yea and Amen, the Bible says in 2 Corinthians 1:20! Do you realize that the Holy Spirit is telling us in this Scripture that every single promise of God is Yea and Amen in Christ Jesus.

All of His promises, not just some of them. What does Yea and Amen mean? It means yes and so be it! It means yes and by all means yes! God is declaring in His precious Word that the answer to every single one of His promises in Christ is Yes and Yes indeed! Is that positive enough for you?

We will look at this Scripture in more depth later - for now, it is enough to know that God designed all of His promises for you - He made His promises to you and He made them for you!

God made His promises to you so you can enjoy His life in your life.

God does not allow sickness or poverty, or grief, or loneliness, or unhappiness, or inadequacy, or any of that junk to dwell in His Kingdom. If He allowed these things in His Kingdom, we would not be delivered out of the power of darkness, would we? We would still be living in the domain of darkness, not in God's Kingdom, and the Bible says we have been delivered from the power of darkness!

Then why are people who are saved still living on wilderness benefits? Why are they living as if they are still wandering around in the wilderness? Some of them act as if they have never even heard of the Promised Land; they do not even seem to know which direction the Promised Land is, let alone possess it!

Why aren't all Christians enjoying the benefits of being children of the King? Does God really have any benefits in this life? Are all of His benefits reserved and postponed to the life to come?

Psalm 103:2 declares:

"BLESS THE LORD, O MY SOUL, AND FORGET NOT ALL HIS BENEFITS."

The Bible says that God has a benefit program. Did you know that? Have you forgotten about His benefits? Are you interested in possessing them? You are interested in eternal life, and peace, and healing, and adequacy, aren't you? Well of course, you are! And God is interested in you participating in His benefit program, because He qualified you to participate.

Colossians 1:12 says:

"God has qualified us as partakers!"

How did God qualify us? He qualified us through Christ! Jesus is your qualification. You were qualified to share in God's benefit program when you received Christ as Savior.

The Next verse, Psalm 103:3, says that God is the One who forgives your iniquities, and who heals all of your diseases. Unfortunately many Believers have never experienced God's benefits in their lives, because the three stooges have been ruling supreme in their sense natures. And they - the 3 stooges - have convinced millions of Christians in every nation under the sun that God's promises are not for today.

The devil will try his best to keep you from experiencing and enjoying God's promises in your life. He will try to keep you from entering into your Promised Land - but thank God - the devil and all his demons put together, do not have the power or the authority to keep you from possessing the promises of God in your life!

We are going to look at some of the Familiar Spirits who have been opposing you. We are going to find out how the spirits who have been trying to keep you on the wrong side of the Jordan River operate, so you can neutralize them with the Word of God!

CHAPTER TWO

WHAT ARE FAMILIAR SPIRITS?

The King James translation of the Bible uses the term "Familiar Spirit" sixteen times. This term refers to a spirit of divination, or to its medium or conjurer. Originally it meant the ritual hole or pit dug in the ground to give underworld spirits access to the practitioner for short periods of time. Later, the term was applied to the spirits who came up out of the hole, and also to the necromancer. A "necromancer" is one who "calls up ghosts or spirits to reveal the future, or one who speaks to the dead."

The term "familiar" is used to describe the alleged spirit of a deceased person, or to a spirit belonging to the family - and since it belonged to the family, this spirit was on intimate terms with the deceased person, and consequently it knew things about that person.

A familiar spirit then, was a spirit who was familiar with that specific person.

A parallel term in Hebrew means "to know, a knowing spirit, one with occult knowledge, a wizard, one who is made wise by contacting the nether world by such a demon." Deuteronomy 18:11 indicates that the same medium might consult a familiar spirit as well as a knowing spirit.

"A familiar spirit is a spirit that is familiar with a person, a place, or a thing."

The meaning has not changed. One of the most descriptive accounts in the Old Testament is in 1 Samuel 28, when Saul sought the counsel of a witch to try to contact Samuel who was dead. The "Witch of Endor, who was the mistress of a Familiar Spirit," expected to call up the spirit she was familiar with - her control spirit. Then when Samuel appeared instead of her Familiar Control Spirit, the Witch was astonished and frightened, and it was only then that she recognized Saul as the King.

1 Chronicles 10:13 lists this visit to the Witch, to the one who possessed a Familiar Spirit, as one of the reasons why Saul was destroyed. The punishment for breaking, or for ignoring God's laws, is great.

Sometimes mediums, witches, conjurers, wizards, and some fortune tellers really do work with familiar spirits, or control spirits. These spirits are familiar with a person, a place, or a thing, and consequently they will have knowledge of a particular person, place, or thing. Now that you know this, You should realize that everyone who has some supernatural knowledge about you is not necessarily of God.

A spirit that is familiar with you has knowledge about you, and this spirit or group of spirits will communicate this knowledge to those whom they serve.

Don't let this shake you up. God gives you some standards by which to judge prophecy (surely you would not go to a fortune teller or to a wizard would you?), and when you apply God's standards to the situations and to the people in your life you will not be fooled.

In the Spirit World your life is just like a history book, so do not be surprised if someone reads a chapter or two in your book and tells you some things that they have no natural way of knowing. The Bible instructs us in Matthew 7:15-20, to be fruit inspectors, so examine the fruit in the lives of the people who are predicting or prophesying to you. If their fruit is rotten, then you will not have any problem in determining their source of information.

It is impossible for a Spiritualist, or a Medium, or a Necromancer, or even for a Prophet of the Lord, to speak to the dead. Those who try to deceive and act as if they can speak to the dead, speak to - and get their information from - spirits who are familiar with a particular person or a situation. When you examine the Scriptures, you understand that no one can call up, or speak to, a deceased person or to their spirit.

Paul, by the inspiration of the Holy Spirit, wrote in 2 Corinthians 5:8:

"...TO BE ABSENT FROM THE BODY IS TO BE PRESENT WITH THE LORD."

Then in Ecclesiastes 12:7 the Holy Spirit recorded:

"...THEN THE DUST WILL RETURN TO THE EARTH AS IT WAS, AND THE SPIRIT WILL RETURN TO GOD WHO GAVE IT."

Luke 16:19-31, records the account of the beggar Lazarus. Lazarus died and went to Abraham's bosom, and then the rich man died, and he went to Hades.

(You do realize that you are going to Heaven or to Hades when you die, don't you?).

The rich man could not cross over to Lazarus, and Lazarus could not cross over to him. Furthermore, Lazarus could not return to earth to warn the rich man's brothers. He could not speak to them or communicate with them in any way.

It is obvious from these Scriptures that no person or thing has the right, or the power, to do anything with your spirit except God. When your body goes to the grave - your spirit - the real you in you, instantly goes to be with the Lord, or goes to the place of torment with the devil.

The account of Lazarus is very interesting because it lets us see just a little into the Spirit World. The rich man in Hades recognized Lazarus whom he knew on earth, and he also recognized Abraham whom he had never seen. This tells us that we are going to recognize, and we are going to be recognized when we are absent from our bodies and present with the Lord. We are going to know, and we are going to be known.

We will recognize our loved ones in Heaven, and they will recognize us. We are also going to recognize the saints of old: Peter, Paul, James, John, David, Isaiah, Joshua, Elijah, Abraham, and all the others. Think about that marvelous fact, we will know all of the inhabitants of Heaven, and all of them will know us.

This account also teaches us that we are going to have feelings in Heaven or in Hell.

The rich man could see, he was thirsty, and he could talk and hear. He still had all of his emotions. He still existed, and he was in torment!

When you die physically, you are not going off somewhere to be a puff of smoke, or a breath of air, or into a grave of nothingness. The real you is in you! The real you is your inner man, and the real you in you is going to live forever. That is why Jesus came, isn't it? The Bible tells us about eternal life in John 3:16. A part of your inheritance is to live forever with the Lord!

You will know and you will be known forever! When you go to be with the Lord, no one can call your spirit, or anyone else's spirit, back and forth like some errand boy. You will be rejoicing in the presence of the Messiah, or burning in the place of torment with the devil! But you will not be running back and forth delivering messages or predictions. You will never be at the beck and call of some necromancer, or witch, or fortune teller. You will be in Paradise with the Lord, or you will be in Hades with the devil!

The final die is cast at death!

CHAPTER THREE

FAMILIAR SPIRITS ARE SPIRITS WHO ARE FAMILIAR WITH YOU

The spirits who have become familiar with me are my Familiar Spirits. They are spirits who are familiar with me. The spirits who are familiar with me, are not necessarily familiar with you, and the spirits who are familiar with you are not familiar with me.

Spirits are familiar with the person they have lived with or around. They become familiar the same way you become familiar, by being around someone. By being closely associated with them.

There are some spirits that are common spirits. That is to say there are some spirits who are found almost every place. They are not limited or confined to a specific area or territory. The three stooges, for instance -

I find this bunch in every part of the country and in every nation I have visited. Spirits attract spirits! That is easy to see when you look at areas like San Francisco, or Las Vegas, or Chicago, or Rome. They are attracted to common groups like the Mafia, or to the Hell's Angels, or to a group of homosexuals, or to any similar group.

An old folk saying is, "Birds of a feather flock together." Spirits operate the same way. They will live where they are welcome or tolerated. They flock together, and if you allow them to "flock" around you they will try to influence you.

Listen to me very carefully, the people you choose to associate with will make a vital life changing difference in your life and in your well being, because the spirits operating in their lives will try to operate in you.

FAMILIAR SPIRITS IN ABRAHAM'S AND ISSAC'S LIVES

Let me show you a Biblical example of how Familiar Spirits work. Genesis 12 records the account of Abraham's call. God spoke to him - He told Abraham what to do, and Abraham did it. The Bible says,

"ABRAHAM BELIEVED GOD, AND GOD IMPUTED UNTO HIM RIGHTEOUSNESS."

Isn't that tremendous! God said, Abraham did; and because he did, God imputed Righteousness unto him. Do you think we might get righteousness imputed the same way today? By believing God? By doing what He says to do? Well, of course we will. In fact, the Bible says in 2 Corinthians 5:21:

"HE MADE HIM WHO KNEW NO SIN TO BE SIN ON OUR BEHALF, THAT WE MIGHT BECOME THE RIGHTEOUSNESS OF GOD IN HIM."

Jesus is our righteousness! And we receive His righteousness by believing God. Thank God, it still works for you and for me just like it did for Abraham.

You have the right to partake of His righteousness because Jesus became a sacrifice for your sins so you might become The Righteousness of God in Him.

Now I want you to read Genesis 12:9-20 with me:

"AND ABRAM JOURNEYED ON, CONTINUING TOWARD THE NEGEV.
NOW THERE WAS A FAMINE IN THE LAND: SO ABRAM WENT DOWN TO EGYPT TO SOJOURN THERE, FOR THE FAMINE WAS SEVERE IN THE LAND. AND IT CAME ABOUT WHEN HE CAME NEAR TO EGYPT, THAT HE SAID TO SARAI HIS WIFE, 'SEE NOW, I KNOW THAT YOU ARE A BEAUTIFUL WOMAN;
AND IT WILL COME ABOUT WHEN THE EGYPTIANS SEE YOU, THAT THEY WILL SAY 'THIS IS HIS WIFE', AND THEY WILL KILL ME, BUT THEY WILL LET YOU LIVE.

PLEASE SAY THAT YOU ARE MY SISTER SO THAT IT MAY GO WELL WITH ME BECAUSE OF YOU, AND THAT I MAY LIVE ON ACCOUNT OF YOU.'

AND IT CAME ABOUT WHEN ABRAM CAME INTO EGYPT, THE EGYPTIANS SAW THAT THE WOMAN WAS VERY BEAUTIFUL.

AND PHARAOH'S OFFICIALS SAW HER AND PRAISED HER TO PHARAOH; AND THE WOMAN WAS TAKEN INTO PHARAOH'S HOUSE.
THEREFORE HE TREATED ABRAM WELL FOR HER SAKE; AND GAVE HIM SHEEP AND OXEN AND DONKEYS AND MALE AND

FEMALE SERVANTS AND FEMALE DONKEYS
AND CAMELS.
BUT THE LORD STRUCK PHARAOH AND HIS
HOUSE WITH GREAT PLAGUES BECAUSE OF
SARAI, ABRAM'S WIFE.
THEN PHARAOH CALLED ABRAM AND SAID,
'WHAT IS THIS YOU HAVE DONE TO ME?
WHY DID YOU NOT TELL ME THAT SHE WAS
YOUR WIFE?

WHY DID YOU SAY SHE IS MY SISTER, SO
THAT I TOOK HER FOR MY WIFE? NOW
THEN, HERE IS YOUR WIFE; TAKE HER AND
GO.'

AND PHARAOH COMMANDED HIS MEN
CONCERNING HIM; AND THEY ESCORTED
HIM AWAY, WITH HIS WIFE AND ALL THAT
BELONGED TO HIM."

Abraham, the friend of God, the man who believed God, the one unto whom God imputed righteousness, got in a tough situation and he was afraid. Then, motivated by fear, he called his wife his sister! This is not a very pleasant account of one of our heroes, is it?

God always tells the truth, and if we will continue studying and meditating on His Word, we will see that the truth was recorded for our benefit.

God wrote the Bible for us; He did not write the Bible for Abraham, or Isaac, or for Jacob; they were already in Paradise when the Bible was written. He had the Bible written for you and for me. One of the reasons that God had His Word recorded is to make us adequate.

Let's look at 2 Timothy 3:16-17 together:

"ALL SCRIPTURE IS INSPIRED BY GOD AND PROFITABLE FOR TEACHING, FOR REPROOF, FOR CORRECTION, FOR TRAINING IN RIGHTEOUSNESS:
THAT THE MAN OF GOD MAY BE ADEQUATE, EQUIPPED FOR EVERY GOOD WORK."

The Bible says all Scripture is inspired by God and that it is profitable. Well, what is profitable about the Scriptures telling us that Abram lied about Sarai? As we study this traumatic experience in Abraham's life, we see that:

1. Abraham was human.
2. He felt like we do sometimes when he faced the mountains in his life.
3. God recorded this story, not to tell all the bad stuff about Abraham, but to instruct us - to teach us how the devil will try to slither into our lives. And when we learn the devil's schemes, we will be adequately prepared to stop him! God's Word equips us to crush the devil's head under our feet!

These Scriptures will be profitable to us as we continue to study Abraham's life.

Now turn with me to Genesis 20, eight chapters and almost 25 years later. Let me read the first 5 verses of this chapter to you.

"NOW ABRAHAM JOURNEYED FROM THERE TOWARD THE LAND OF THE NEGEV, AND SETTLED BETWEEN KADESH AND SHUR; AND HE SOJOURNED IN GERAR.

AND ABRAHAM SAID OF SARAH HIS WIFE,
'SHE IS MY SISTER.' SO ABIMELECH KING
OF GERAR SENT AND TOOK SARAH.

BUT GOD CAME TO ABIMELECH IN A DREAM
OF THE NIGHT, AND SAID TO HIM, 'BEHOLD,
YOU ARE A DEAD MAN BECAUSE OF THE
WOMAN WHOM YOU HAVE TAKEN, FOR SHE
IS MARRIED.' NOW ABIMELECH HAD NOT
COME NEAR HER; AND HE SAID, 'LORD,
WILT THOU SLAY A NATION, EVEN THOUGH
BLAMELESS?'

'DID HE NOT HIMSELF SAY TO ME, SHE IS
MY SISTER? AND SHE HERSELF SAID, HE IS
MY BROTHER.' "

In this account we see that Abram's name had been
changed to Abraham, and Sarai's name had been
changed to Sarah. They had lived in the Promised
Land for almost 25 years now, and they knew God.
They served Him and they knew His Faithfulness. The
Lord changed their names when He promised them a
heir again in Genesis 17 - but regardless of the name
change - the same spirits were still operating in their
lives. Abimelech said in verse 5,

"DID HE NOT HIMSELF SAY TO ME, SHE IS
MY SISTER? AND SHE HERSELF SAID, HE IS
MY BROTHER."

We know that verse 12 of this chapter says that
Sarah was his half sister since both of them had the

same father. But the truth of the matter was - Sarah was not functioning as his sister - she was his wife! The amazing thing in this account is that both of them told the King that Sarah was his sister.

They lied!

The same spirits that were operating in Abraham's life in Chapter 12, were now operating in Sarah. In this account, Sarah told the same lie Abraham told.

The same spirit that caused Abraham to lie, also caused Sarah to lie! Are you beginning to see how these spirits work? When they are around you, they will try to influence your life - they will try to control you. They will do their best to become familiar with you, so they can try to run and then ruin your life.

Do you remember the account of Ananias and his wife Sapphira in Acts 5? Ananias lied about how much money they sold their property for, and Peter said in Acts 5:3,

"WHY HAS SATAN FILLED YOUR HEART TO LIE TO THE HOLY SPIRIT...?"

Then after Ananias died, his wife Sapphira came in and told the same lie. Why? Because they were controlled by the same spirit! A lying spirit from the devil was working in their family, and that spirit influenced Sapphira, and caused her to tell the same lie her husband told! Just as Sarah told the same lie Abraham told.

When you know that your spouse - or anyone else for that matter - is lying or deceiving, or doing wrong, have enough of God's wisdom not to partake of their sins. If you partake with them, you will also reap with them.

1Corinthians 15:33 declares:

**"DO NOT BE DECEIVED, BAD COMPANY
CORRUPTS GOOD MORALS."**

In Proverbs 4:23 the Lord instructs us:

**"WATCH OVER YOUR HEART WITH ALL
DILIGENCE, FOR FROM IT FLOW THE
SPRINGS OF LIFE."**

Many times we choose our destiny by the people
with whom we choose to associate. Bad company
does corrupt good morals! It is vital that you
understand this basic Biblical principle. If you
associate with those who have bad morals, the spirits
operating in their lives will try to drag you down to their
level.

You must watch over your heart with all diligence,
and you must put a guard on your mind and on your
mouth.

You can fix your destiny for bad by selecting
ding-a-ling companions.

THE BIRTH OF ISAAC

Let's see how these Spirits continued to work in this
family. God kept all of His promises to His friend
Abraham, and at the proper time the son of the Promise
was born. God's faithfulness was further
demonstrated when He revealed Himself to Abraham
on Mt. Moriah as JEHOVAH JIREH, the God who
provides; when He provided the ram in the bush for a
sacrifice.

Sarah died and was buried at Machpelah (in Hebron). Isaac grew up and the Lord gave him Rebekah as a wife. Then Abraham died, and Isaac was the head of the one family on earth that God had chosen and promised to bless.

Isaac was the seed of Abraham! His wife, Rebekah, bore him two sons, Jacob and Esau. Isaac knew God, and God continued to bless him. Now let's read Genesis 26:1, 6-7:

"NOW THERE WAS A FAMINE IN THE LAND, BESIDES THE PREVIOUS FAMINE THAT HAD OCCURRED IN THE DAYS OF ABRAHAM. SO ISAAC WENT TO GERAR, TO ABIMELECH KING OF THE PHILISTINES.

SO ISAAC LIVED IN GERAR.
WHEN THE MEN OF THE PLACE ASKED ABOUT HIS WIFE, HE SAID, 'SHE IS MY SISTER,' FOR HE WAS AFRAID TO SAY, 'MY WIFE,' THINKING, THE MEN OF THE PLACE MIGHT KILL ME ON ACCOUNT OF REBEKAH, FOR SHE IS BEAUTIFUL."

Did you notice that Isaac did exactly the same thing his father did? He lied! In verse 7 Isaac said,

"SHE IS MY SISTER!"

Isaac called his wife, his sister. Why would he do that? Would you? Do you know anyone who would? Of course not. No man in the natural would say that his wife was his sister if he knew that as a result of his declaration - his wife would end up in a king's harem! Then why did Abraham and Isaac lie about their wives?

Because they were influenced by spirits!

Isaac was not even born when his father called his wife his sister. In fact, more that 40 years had passed since Abraham lied about Sarah, but Isaac did the exact same thing his father did when he was in a similar situation.

Isaac was Abraham's son. He grew up in Abraham's family, and the same spirit that caused his father to lie, became familiar with him, and that spirit caused Isaac to lie.

These lying, deceiving spirits became familiar with Isaac because they lived with him. They were in his family. They were around him as he grew up! That is the way spirits become familiar with you, by living in the same family with you, or by being around you.

Isaac knew that the Lord was a provider, he was on Mt Moriah also, remember? He knew God was a supernatural God, and he knew that he had a special relationship with the Lord. But regardless of all this good stuff, at this particular point in his life, when he faced a crisis - The same spirits who had influenced his father and his mother, also influenced him. They had attached themselves to him - they had became familiar with him while he was growing up.

Doesn't that startle you?

The same spirits that caused Abraham to lie, also caused Sarah to lie. And now over forty years after his parents lied, these spirits caused their son Isaac to tell the same lie!

You can see how spirits work. The spirits you are around will try to become familiar with you and influence your life. The spirits that worked in Abraham's life, became familiar with Isaac and they caused the son of the Promise to lie.

This is perhaps the most dramatic example of how these lying and deceiving spirits operated in Abraham's family. But it is not the only example. Look at how they continued to operate in this family, long after Abraham was dead.

Abraham lied about Sarah to Pharaoh and to Abimelech.

Isaac lied to Abimelech about Rebekah when he said, "She is my sister." Isaac taught Rebekah how to deceive when he lied and said she was his sister, and then she taught their son Jacob to deceive. Rebekah was the one who told Jacob to cover his arms with goat skin and lie to Isaac - to say, "Hey dad, my name is Easu." - to deceive him so he would think that he was Easu, so that he, Jacob, could receive the first-born's birthright.
(The devil will always give you many good reasons to lie and deceive.)
Some of these same spirits attached themselves to Jacob and traveled with him when he went to Haran, where Laban was both willing and able to deceive him. And Laban did just that, he deceived Jacob when he gave Leah to him as his wife instead of Rachel. The Bible says you always reap what you sow! Jacob reaped, and so will you.

Years later Jacob's sons lied to him and deceived him about Joseph's death after they had sold Joseph to the Ishmaelite traders, who took him to Egypt.

Listen to me carefully now, spirits do not die! People die, but the spirits who operated in their lives will continue to try to influence the lives of the people they are around until these spirits are overcome and defeated by the Word of God.

CHAPTER FOUR

GOD FORGIVES AND FORGETS!

Let me digress just a little, and point out something that is vitally important for every Believer to realize. Have you ever noticed that the failures and the sins of God's people in the Old Testament, are not recorded in the New Testament? Abraham's and Sarah's and Isaac's lies, David's adultery and murder, Sampson's wantonness? God does not talk about them in the New Testament.

Have you ever wondered why?

Well, it is because their problems, their iniquities, all of their sins, all of their mistakes, and all of their weaknesses - are under the blood! When they asked for forgiveness they were washed clean by the blood of the Lamb of God that was shed at Calvary.

God forgave them, and when He forgave them, He forgot about their transgressions. That is what the Bible says in Isaiah 43:25:

"I, EVEN I, AM THE ONE WHO WIPES OUT YOUR TRANSGRESSIONS FOR MY OWN SAKE, AND I WILL NOT REMEMBER YOUR SINS."

God does not remember forgiven sins. Isn't that tremendous! God forgives and then God forgets about your sins!

The blood of the Lamb has released us from our sins (Revelation 1:5). We have been released, and since we have been released, that means we have been set free! We are no longer held in bondage by sin! It is vital that you understand this basic precept of God's forgiveness through His Son. When you ask for forgiveness, God forgives you and then He forgets all about your sin. He is not counting your trespasses against you.

God does not remember forgiven sins!

The only ones who remember your sin is you, the devil, and sometimes the Church. As long as the devil can get you to concentrate on the mistakes you have made in your life - the bad! - You will never feel worthy enough to receive the good God has planned for you. The accuser of the brethren will accuse you of your sins, he will remind you of your failures, and he will do his very best to convince you that you are not worthy enough for anything good to ever happen to you.

The next time the devil comes around reminding you about something that is under the blood in your life, just quote Isaiah 43:25 to him and then reinforce it with 1 John 1:9:

"IF WE CONFESS OUR SINS, HE IS FAITHFUL AND RIGHTEOUS TO FORGIVE OUR SINS AND TO CLEANSE US FROM ALL UNRIGHTEOUSNESS."

Thank God He forgives and He forgets, and you must do the same! After you have been restored to favor with the Father, after you have repented and have been forgiven, do not dwell on your shortcomings and failures. Be determined to go on in the love of the Lord, and with His help you can get your life together. The

Bible tells you in Hebrews 12:2 to Keep your eyes fixed on Jesus, not on your failures and the mistakes you made in the past. If you continue to live in the past, your future will always be the same as your past. That means your history will be your future, and your future is your past. Think about that. So if you want your future to be better than your past, you must follow the Biblical instructions to keep your eyes on Jesus!

By the way, you will have to apply these same principles to your life - when you forgive someone, you must forget about their trespasses.

Sometimes I hear people say, "Well, I'll forgive them all right, but I will never forget about what they have done." That will not work! That is not Biblical! God forgives and forgets, and if you want His forgiveness, you too, must forgive and forget. Don't try to do it on your own, ask the Lord to give you amnesia about the wrongs or hurts that others have done to you.

If you need some Scripture for this, try Mark 11:25-26, where the Lord said,

"AND WHENEVER YOU STAND PRAYING, FORGIVE, IF YOU HAVE ANYTHING AGAINST ANYONE; SO THAT YOUR FATHER ALSO WHO IS IN HEAVEN MAY FORGIVE YOU YOUR TRANSGRESSIONS.
BUT IF YOU DO NOT FORGIVE, NEITHER WILL YOUR FATHER WHO IS IN HEAVEN FORGIVE YOUR TRANSGRESSIONS."

Jesus said, "If you do not forgive, God will not forgive you." That is very plain, isn't it.

And in Matthew 6:12, when you pray the Lord's Prayer, Jesus taught you to pray,

"FORGIVE US OUR DEBTS AS WE FORGIVE OUR DEBTORS."

Is that really the way you want to pray? Do you want God to give you the same amount of forgiveness you give others? Have you thought that through? When you realize this Biblical truth, you will forgive everyone fully and completely. To receive God's forgiveness you must forgive others, and Biblical forgiveness always includes forgetfulness.

What if God remembered all of your sins and reminded you of them every day or two? You would be a mess, wouldn't you? You would never feel worthy or adequate. Your mind would always be re-running your mistakes and failures, and you would constantly be living in and being controlled by your past, and you would not accomplish anything positive.

You have to forgive yourself, then you have to forget about your trespasses. You have to forgive others, and then you have to forget about their trespasses against you.

What does all this mean? It means you have to disregard the bad that others have done to you!

Do you know that God does not have a plan of salvation for elephants? That is true! Do you know why? It is because elephants never forget. They remember a hurt or a wrong forever, and then they always get even, even if it takes them 50 years or so. If their trainer does something bad to them when they were just a little baby elephant, they remember it all of their lives; until finally, one day, they pick up a tent stake and use it on his head. They get even!

There are a lot of church members like that today; they cannot forget the wrong or hurt, real or imagined, that someone has done to them. Their relationship with the Lord is disrupted - totally derailed! - Not necessarily because of the wrong that was done, but because they could not, or they would not, do what the Word of God tells them to do. They refuse to forgive and to forget.

Let me share an example to illustrate this point. I was ministering in a service in Columbus, Ohio, and a lady came forward for prayer who was full of fear. I prayed for her and rebuked the spirit of fear, but she did not get any relief. When I looked at her, I could see that she was still full of trouble. When relief does not come after prayer, you need to probe deeper to see if there is some basic underlying problem that is hindering God's power from working. I asked her, "Do you have ought against anyone?"

When I said that her face began to cloud up. She began to cry a little and said, "It's my husband, I cannot forgive my husband." As I ministered to her, I learned her husband had left her 14 long years before, and she had never been able to forgive him. Finally her unforgiveness had consumed her, it had destroyed her life.

She had accommodated unforgiveness in her life for so long that that spirit had invited fear in, and now fear ruled her life. She was afraid of everything. Fear is fearful! Unforgiveness is a destroyer!

Her ex-husband had remarried long ago, and perhaps he had forgotten all about her, but she had not forgotten all the hurt he had caused her. She had nursed the hurt - she babied it - she pampered it - and she gave in to it - until finally it had grown up to be a full grown monster! And now unforgiveness and fear were the dominant emotions in her life. These spirits ruled in her life, and they made her life miserable.

Oh, what a tragedy it is if you allow this spirit to build a stronghold in you. Get rid of unforgiveness! It eats away at you like leprosy, and in a moment of crisis - just when you need to reach the Lord on a vital matter - a cactus patch of unforgiveness will pop up in your heart and you will not be able to receive the petition you are presenting. Get rid of it! Cast unforgiveness out of your life - do not nurse it any longer. Ask God to help you to forgive!

Let me remind you of something else. Since God has forgiven and forgotten your transgressions, that means that no minister of the Lord will know about them. God cannot reveal the sins of your past to anyone when they are under the blood of the Lamb. He cannot reveal them to any of His ministers by the Word of Knowledge, or by Prophesy, or by any other gift of the Spirit, because God has forgotten about your sins! Remember - God forgives and He forgets.

What does all this mean? This means that if anyone begins to tell you that God has shown them something about your past that is under the blood of the Lamb - something that you have asked for God's forgiveness - then you can be sure that it is not God who is showing them your past. So they only have two possible sources for their information, if it is accurate. Some gossip in the church has told them about you, or they have been in communication (dealing) with the devil.

Let me remind you again that when you are forgiven, the only ones who remember your sin is you, the devil, and sometimes the church! If anyone tries to put a Supernatural Shuck on you by saying that God has revealed your sinful past to them, and if you have been forgiven for that particular thing, then be assured that they are not getting their information from the Lord. Get away from them, and stay away from them!

They are not serving the Lord who saves, heals, and forgives sins, because He forgot all about your sins when you became a new creature!

CHAPTER FIVE

CAN THE DEVIL READ YOUR MIND?

That is a major question, isn't it? Does the devil know what you are thinking? Many Christians think that the devil knows their every thought, that he can read their minds, and that he just possibly may be holding their future in the palm of his hand. We need to find out if this is true or not.

Can the devil read your mind? Does he know what you are thinking?

Why do some people think that the devil can read their minds anyway? Generally, it is because of the things that happen in their lives. It just seems like he knows their thoughts sometimes.

Let's begin to explore this question by looking at what Familiar Spirits are and how they work. Familiar Spirits are spirits who are familiar with you. They know how you act, and they know how you react to almost every situation. They know about you because they have lived with you, or around you for years. They have become familiar with you!

Have you ever heard a wife say to her husband, "I know you better than you know yourself." How did she get to know her husband better that he knows himself? Did she know him better than he knew himself before they got married? No! She got to know him by living with him. Whether she really knows her husband better than he knows himself is not material, she certainly knows him much better after she married him than she knew him before they were married.

Well, that is the same way familiar spirits get their knowledge about you. They have lived with you or they have been around you for so long, that they know exactly what it takes to turn you on, or to turn you off - they know what makes you mad, and they also know what makes you sad. They know how to get you down! They know how to stack up the circumstantial evidence in your life until the negative evidence gets so bad that you almost want to give up in despair.

That is why some people think the devil can read their minds, because those old familiar spirits who have been hanging around them know how to get their "Goats," and when they do, that person thinks, "Oh, the devil knows just what I am thinking, it is no use," and they give up.

Let me assure you, the devil cannot read your mind! And in addition to assuring you of this, I want to give you the Biblical documentation.

Frequently, many Christians have almost automatically assumed, through lack of knowledge, that the devil has the attributes of God. That is nonsense, but it is a favorite lie of the devil! God spoke through His prophet in Hosea 4:6 and said:

"MY PEOPLE ARE DESTROYED FOR LACK OF KNOWLEDGE."

Was this Scripture recorded just for the people who lived in the Old Testament? Surely God is not talking about the current bunch of Believers is He? Was this Scripture recorded for the ones who hear His Word on radio and on TV? - For the ones who have all these teaching tapes and attend teaching seminars? Is the

Church really being destroyed today for lack of knowledge of what God's Word says and means?

Of course it is! The devil is a deceiver, and if he can deceive you into thinking that you do not have to know and practice God's Word, then he has got you in a heap of trouble. If you base your life on experiences rather than on what God's Word says, you never will be an overcomer. You should underline that thought.

I have never had anyone come up to me in a prayer line and say, "Please pray that I will continue to have a lack of knowledge, so I can be destroyed." That is foolishness, isn't it? If someone ever did that, I would probably begin to pray that the Lord would manifest a sound mind for them, or I might even put in a quick call for the guys in the white suits who carry nets and straight jackets around with them.

But many Christians are being destroyed for a lack of knowledge - They are being destroyed because they refuse to find out what God's Word says about the problems they are having in their lives, and consequently they are eventually destroyed because they do not know how to deal with these problems.

Aren't you glad this is not your prognosis?

You are not going to be destroyed for lack of knowledge, because you are going to learn God's Word. Say that with me, will you? "I am a learner! I am learning God's Word! I am not going to be destroyed for lack of knowledge!"

The devil does not have God's attributes or abilities. Let me share a few things that the devil is not.

THE DEVIL IS NOT OMNIPOTENT!

He does not have unlimited power, that belongs only to God. Jesus said in Matthew 28:18

"ALL AUTHORITY (POWER) HAS BEEN GIVEN TO ME IN HEAVEN AND ON EARTH."

The devil does not have power or authority over The Lord Jesus Christ, and since you are in Christ, and Christ is in you, the devil does not have power over you.

That does not mean that the devil will not try to dominate you. He will try! - But you can stop him when you learn God's Word.

THE DEVIL IS NOT OMNIPRESENT!

The devil does not have the power to be present everywhere at the same time. He is a created being, and he is limited to occupying one place at one time.

God is the only one who has the power to be equally present every place.

Jesus said in Matthew 18:20,

"WHERE TWO OR THREE OF YOU ARE GATHERED TOGETHER IN MY NAME, THERE WILL I BE IN THE MIDST OF YOU."

The Father, the Son, and the Holy Spirit are equally present in every place all of the time.

Do you remember in Luke 10:18 when the 70 returned to the Lord rejoicing that the demons were subject to them, and Jesus said,

"I BEHELD SATAN AS LIGHTNING FALL FROM HEAVEN."

If the devil was every place, could he fall from some particular place?

Revelation 12:7-9 records that Michael and his angels fought against the dragon,

"...AND THE GREAT DRAGON WAS CAST OUT, THAT OLD SERPENT, CALLED THE DEVIL AND SATAN, WHICH DECEIVED THE WHOLE WORLD..."

The devil was cast out! To be cast out he had to be some place.

Has he deceived you into thinking that he is like God? That is the reason he fell in the first place, isn't it? Didn't he want to be like the Most High God? The devil wanted to take God's place and God's throne.

That is what the Bible says in Isaiah 14:12-17. Do you realize that he has achieved his goal in your life; that he has accomplished his primary purpose, if he has convinced you

that he is all powerful,
that he is equally present everywhere,
and that he knows every thing,
that he is just like God!

THE DEVIL IS NOT OMNISCIENCE!

He does not know everything. This is an attribute of God. God the Creator knows all things, not the devil.

The devil does not know what is in your mind!

We need to look at a few examples. Do you remember when the Holy Ghost sent Paul and Baranabas on their first missionary journey in Acts 13? Let's join them in Acts 13:6:

"AND WHEN THEY HAD GONE THROUGH THE WHOLE ISLAND AS FAR AS PAPHOS, THEY FOUND A CERTAIN MAGICIAN, A JEWISH FALSE PROPHET WHOSE NAME WAS BAR-JESUS,
WHO WAS WITH THE PROCONSUL, SERGIUS PAULUS, A MAN OF INTELLIGENCE. THIS MAN SUMMONED BARNABAS AND SAUL AND SOUGHT TO HEAR THE WORD OF GOD.

BUT ELYMAS, THE MAGICIAN (FOR THUS HIS NAME IS TRANSLATED), WAS OPPOSING THEM, SEEKING TO TURN THE PROCONSUL AWAY FROM THE FAITH. BUT SAUL, WHO WAS ALSO KNOWN AS PAUL, FILLED WITH THE HOLY SPIRIT, FIXED HIS GAZE UPON HIM, AND SAID, 'YOU WHO ARE FULL OF ALL DECEIT AND FRAUD, YOU SON OF THE DEVIL, YOU ENEMY OF ALL RIGHTEOUSNESS, WILL YOU NOT CEASE TO MAKE CROOKED THE STRAIGHT WAYS OF THE LORD?
AND NOW BEHOLD, THE HAND OF THE LORD IS UPON YOU, AND YOU WILL BE BLIND AND NOT SEE THE SUN FOR A TIME.'
AND IMMEDIATELY A MIST AND A DARKNESS FELL UPON HIM AND HE WENT ABOUT SEEKING THOSE WHO WOULD LEAD HIM BY THE HAND."

Do you realize that this man, who the Holy Ghost caused Paul to call the Son of the Devil, the enemy of all righteousness - did not know what Paul was going to do! He could not read his mind.

Don't you think if the devil could read minds, or if he knew the future, that he would have read Paul's mind and then he would have known that Paul was going to rebuke his servant openly? Surely, if the devil had known what was going to happen, if he had known the future, he would have snatched this Bar-Jesus, his son, out of the combat zone.

Let's look at another confrontation Paul had with the devil in Acts 16 starting with verse 16,

> "AND IT HAPPENED THAT AS WE WERE GOING TO THE PLACE OF PRAYER, A CERTAIN SLAVE GIRL, HAVING A SPIRIT OF DIVINATION MET US, WHO WAS BRINGING HER MASTERS MUCH PROFIT BY FORTUNE-TELLING.
> FOLLOWING AFTER PAUL AND US, SHE KEPT CRYING OUT SAYING, 'THESE MEN ARE BOND SERVANTS OF THE MOST HIGH GOD, WHO ARE PROCLAIMING TO YOU THE WAY OF SALVATION.' AND SHE CONTINUED DOING THIS FOR MANY DAYS. BUT PAUL WAS GREATLY ANNOYED, AND TURNED AND SAID TO THE SPIRIT, 'I COMMAND YOU IN THE NAME OF JESUS CHRIST TO COME OUT OF HER!' AND IT CAME OUT AT THAT VERY MOMENT."

If the devil, through the spirit of divination, or through any other spirit - or by any other power - could have read Paul's mind, or if he had known the future, he would not have allowed one of his spirits to be cast out of that girl and defeated!

The devil did not know what Paul was going to do! And when Paul commanded the spirit to come out of the girl, the devil did not have the power to resist him!

That spirit did not shout "I am not coming out! I refuse!"

The devil and every other spirit is subject to the name of Jesus, and when Paul spoke to him using the Name that is above every name, that spirit obeyed. It did not have a choice, it came out!

The devil does not know all! He cannot read your mind! And he is not all powerful!

Do you remember when Jesus was tempted by the devil in the wilderness? Do you think that if the devil had been able to read Jesus' mind, or if he had known His thoughts - or if he had known the future - that he would have challenged Jesus to turn the stones into bread, or to cast Himself off the pinnacle of the temple, or to fall down and worship him? Would he have gone on to certain defeat? Would he have tried all of his tricks if he had known that he was going to be defeated every time?

You need to realize that the Bible plainly teaches that the devil cannot read your mind, and furthermore, that he does not know your future. He did not know Jesus' future; he did not know Paul's future; and thank God, he does not know your future.

You know that the devil did not know his own future or he never would have rebelled in the first place. He would still be serving God.

The devil could not read Jesus's mind, and he cannot read yours. The Bible says in Philippians 2:5,

"LET THIS MIND BE IN YOU WHICH WAS ALSO IN CHRIST JESUS."

That is what it says. Read it in your Bible! You have the right to have the mind of Christ, and if the devil could not read Jesus' mind in the wilderness, or Paul's mind in Philippi, do not let any junky teaching or your lack of knowledge convince you that the devil can read your mind wherever you are today.

1 Corinthians 2:11 declares,

"FOR WHO AMONG MEN KNOWS THE THOUGHTS OF A MAN EXCEPT THE SPIRIT OF THE MAN WHICH IS IN HIM."

Who can know your thoughts? Why, your own spirit and the Spirit that God put in you. When you were born again you did get God's Spirit, didn't you? Of course, you did. John 14:23 says that the Father and the Son came to live in you. Christ comes to live in you when you receive Him as your Savior, and God knows your thoughts. He knows your innermost being, He knows everyone's thoughts.

But your thoughts are privileged information, and thank God the devil is not privileged to have this information!

Want to look at one more example? Do you remember in Matthew 2 when the wise men who were following the Star came to worship the Lord, and they made inquiries in Jerusalem of Herod the King? Well, Herod wanted them to come back when they found the New King, and tell him where He was. Herod intended to kill Jesus, and God knew his intentions.

Herod's thoughts were not a secret to God, so He warned the Wise men in a dream not to return to Herod, and they departed for their own country by another way. Herod was in a rage when the Wise men did not return. And because he wanted to kill the Lord, he sent to Bethlehem and slew all the male children from two years old and under.

Herod killed all of these children in error, because he did not know which one was Jesus, and the devil did not know either or he would have told him.

In fact, I am convinced that the devil lost track of Jesus after He fled to Egypt, and he did not know where He was until He was baptized in the Jordan River by John the Baptist. There was not any doubt about who Jesus was when the Heavens opened and the Holy Spirit descended upon Him like a Dove, and God spoke out of Heaven and said:

"THIS IS MY BELOVED SON, IN WHOM I AM WELL PLEASED."

Even I would have known who He was then - and, of course, so did the devil.

The devil cannot read your mind, he does not know everything, he does not have all power, he cannot be in two places at the same time. He is limited in time, in knowledge, and in space. He is in his headquarters - wherever that is, and he operates through his kingdom of demons and fallen angels.

Why then do people think the devil can read their minds? It is because the Familiar Spirits who have been hanging around them much of their lives have knowledge about them. They have been living around them, just like some of them have been living around you and with you for so long that they know how you are going to react to almost every situation.

They are familiar with you!
They have seen you in action before.
They know exactly what will cause you to read someone off;
They know the things that will discourage you;

They know what will make you pout or cry, or blow your top,
or make you feel rejected.

But they cannot read your mind, and they do not know your thoughts!

The only thing the devil knows about you is,

he knows your life-style -
that means he knows your history - and he knows the way you are living now, and he knows what you tell him with your mouth. You need to realize that your actions and your tongue give you away every single time.

The devil has a spirit reporting to him who is familiar with you, and when this spirit has seen you react to certain situations the same way time and time again, he is fairly certain that you will react the same way the next time that situation or a similar situation arises. So he lays the bad stuff on you.

Oh, I know some of you try to fool him the same way you try to fool your spouses or the people in your Church sometimes. A good example of this is after you have heard a message or two on confession, and you are sick, and you want to be healed. You remember what you have heard about Isaiah 53, and you begin to confess that you are healed. (Thank God confession does bring possession to you when you believe in your heart.) Maybe you stand up in Church and say,

"Oh, I believe every word in the Bible. I believe the Bible from cover to cover, from Genesis to Revelation. I believe that by Jesus' stripes I am healed."

Then at the first pain, when old slewfoot zings you with a fiery dart of hurt, you run home, fall down on your bed, pull the covers up over your head, and begin to cry! Why, you have not fooled the devil. He has you figured out, and you can be certain that he is going to continue to use you for target practice, because he still has that same old familiar spirit reporting the damage his fiery darts are doing in your life.

The way some fortune-tellers work, by the way, is by talking with the spirits who are familiar with you. Most fortune-tellers and mediums and the other spooks are just hokus pokus, they do not know anything specific. They tell people things that are common to people who have characteristics that are similar to theirs. They speak in generalities. False prophets do the same thing.

Did you note in Acts 16 that the girl who had a spirit of divination, the one who made her masters lots of money by telling people their future, did not know her own future?

If this fortune-teller in Acts 16 did not know her own future, why would you let the devil lie to you about your future?

The devil does not know your future. But he does know some things - the devil knows the tricks and the schemes he is going to try to pull on you in the future, and he may even know the people and the circumstance that he is going to use to try to defeat you. But he does not know how you are going to react to the temptations he is designing especially for you!

Remember, the only thing the devil knows about you for sure is your history, he knows what you say, and he can see the way you act. Your life- style tells him everything he needs to know about you! But he cannot read your mind.

The way you live your life tells the devil whether you are "abiding in the vine," or not.

CHAPTER SIX

HOW ARE FAMILIAR SPIRITS MANIFESTED?

Let's take a look at how Familiar Spirits work in peoples' lives, so you will know how to handle them when they pop up in your life. You saw what happened to Isaac in Genesis 26. This is their pattern, their M.O.:

They will attach themselves to family groups, or to groups who associate closely together!

Have you ever noticed a girl who is just like her mother? Maybe it is her temper, or her pride, maybe it is her sharp tongue, or her saucy attitude. Maybe it is her "Pity, pity, poor me" spirit. Have you said, "Why, she acts just like her mother!" Thank God she can manifest good spirits, too. It might be her sweet disposition, or her attitude, her willingness to do for others.

There are more good spirits than there are bad spirits, but since the primary purpose of this book is to teach you about Spiritual Warfare, I am going to concentrate on the familiar evil spirits.

"Like father, like son!"

I'm sure that you have heard that expression. Perhaps you have seen a son who acted just like his father. They may have the same walk, or the same arrogance, the same drinking habits, or the same violent temper. It may be the same pattern of running around on their wives. They have the same basic characteristics.

All of these things are caused by spirits. Spirits will try to attach themselves to you. They want to become familiar with you, and when they do, they will try to control your life.

I grew up in Oklahoma, and when I was a child there was a family who lived even farther out in the country than I did, who took revenge for a real or for an imagined wrong, by burning property - houses, barns, fields, or woods. They were burners! They burned anything that would burn. Everyone knew it after awhile, and when there was a fire, the father of this family was the prime suspect. When the dad died, and there was a fire in our area, guess who got the blame? The son, of course, and many times he was the guilty party.

He became a burner because the same spirit that caused his father to burn, caused him to burn. This spirit attached itself to him while he was growing up, while he was a baby, and babies are defenseless!

My wife grew up in South Carolina, in an area where they had strong windstorms from the hurricanes and gales off the Atlantic Coast, and her father was afraid of these storms. Well, she grew up afraid of storms!

The same spirit that caused her father to be afraid, caused her to be afraid. Wherever we lived, when a few thunderclouds blew up, when a storm began to brew, she became frightened. Thank God when she began to study God's Word she learned her rights in Christ, and then she took control of the spirit that had become familiar with her, and she sent it on its way.

Fear is a spirit. The Bible says in 2 Timothy 1:7,

"FOR GOD HATH NOT GIVEN US THE SPIRIT OF FEAR: BUT OF POWER, AND OF LOVE, AND OF A SOUND MIND."

God has not, He hath not, and He will not give you a Spirit of Fear! You need to recognize, if you do not know it already, that fear is caused by a spirit. If you have a spirit of fear operating in your life, it did not come from God, it came from the pits of Hell!

The Greek word translated here as fear is "DEILIA," which according to Vines' Expository Dictionary of New Testament Words, literally means "FEARFULNESS." This word denotes cowardice and timidity, and it is never used in a good sense. The Spirit of Fear comes from the devil, and to get rid of it you must apply God's Word to it and to your life.

Let me share another example about inherited or family spirits. I have a friend in the ministry and the inferior spirits that have made her feel inadequate much of her life, attached themselves to her son, and now he has the same feelings of inadequacy and inferiority that have plagued his mother.

The inferior-inadequacy spirit seems to attach itself to others very easily.

The spirits that control the parents frequently control the children, and many times the manifestations of these spirits in the second generation are much worse than in the first.

Spirits will do their best to become familiar with you. They want to dominate and control your life. Thank God there is a balm in Gilead though, because every spirit is subject to the Name that is above every name; and they, each and every one of these spirits, can be cast out of your life, and out of the lives of your loved ones, by the Word of God.

Remember Hosea 4:6 "MY PEOPLE ARE DESTROYED FOR LACK OF KNOWLEDGE." Frequently when we quote this Scripture we emphasize the negative connotation that is clearly meant. And it is true - if you do not have knowledge of what the Lord has recorded in His Word - and an understanding of what God's Word means - you will be destroyed. If you refuse to learn about God's plan of salvation - you will not be saved. If you do not learn about His healing plan - you will not receive supernatural healing - because there is a lack of knowledge about this part of His plan in your life.

If you have a lack of knowledge about the Lord's adequacy in you - His happiness - His peace - or any of His other marvelous provisions - then the devil has an opportunity to destroy that portion of your life because of your lack of knowledge about God's provisions.

But have you ever meditated on the positive aspects of Hosea 4:6? Do you realize that the devil cannot destroy you, or any part of your life, if you have knowledge of what God's Word says about you! Revelation knowledge of the Word - Revelation knowledge means that His Word is revealed to you! His Word becomes real to you.

That is what we are studying in this book - Revelation Knowledge of how spirits operate, and Revelation Knowledge on how you can defeat them. When you have God's knowledge in your life, you can not be defeated! Hallelujah!

Let's see how these spirits act.

WHAT TO LOOK FOR!

Spirits are passed along from one member of the family, or from one member of a closely related group, to another. Babies or children, natural children as well as spiritual children, have very little resistance, and it is relatively easy for a spirit to attach itself to a child or to a baby Christian, unless someone is covering that baby with prayer.

Let me list a few of the "Heredity" spirits that I see frequently: Fear of the dark, alcoholism, migraine headaches, self pity, dope addiction, epilepsy, sugar diabetes, rebellion, know it all spirits, fear, inadequacy, nerve conditions, stubbornness, and the list goes on and on.

Many of the diseases that are commonly called hereditary are caused by spirits that have attached themselves to that particular family, or group.

Spirits do not die - people die but the spirits will live on and on creating the same problems. Do you know that they will continue to create problems in your life, or in the lives of your loved ones, until you recognize them for what they are, and learn how to defeat them with the Word of God!

That is the reason the Bible instructs us in James 4:7 to:

"SUBMIT THEREFORE TO GOD. RESIST THE DEVIL AND HE WILL FLEE FROM YOU."

The devil is not irresistible - he is resistible! He does not have the right to mess around in your life or in the lives of your loved ones! So submit yourself to God and learn enough of His Word so you can send the devil and all of his spirits on their way.

How do you submit to God? You submit to God by submitting to His Word. You submit to His Word when you become a doer of the Word and not a hearer only.

When you begin to examine family groups or groups who associate closely, you will be amazed to see the same general group of spirits operating in their lives.

Jealousy, rebellion, strife, sickness, insecurity, deception - when you see these spirits in operation, realize that they come from the devil, and then learn how to deal with the specific spirit that is causing the problem with the Word of God, rather than fighting with the symptoms.

When you see the same spirits being manifested in your spouse's life that are in operation in your life, or when you see these spirits beginning to operate in your childrens' lives, you must take control of them, or your loved ones will end up with the same set of problems you have, and many times their problems will be even more severe.

Spirits are always the same, they do not change from one generation to another. Some of the spirits that I see manifested more frequently than others are:

Rebellion - insecurity - (in fact, this spirit is so prevalent that I have added a section to this book entitled "Inadequacy Spirits" so I can set forth their methods of operation more fully) - adultery, alcoholism, fear and strife!

These spirits attach themselves to babies - natural as well as spiritual - that means real babies as well as baby Christians, and soon these spirits become strong enough to begin to operate in their lives.

If the father is an adulterer, many times the son will be an adulterer. If the father is an alcoholic, the son will be an alcoholic. If the mother is a gossip, many times the daughter is a gossip. If the mother is emotional, the daughter will be emotional.

Now this is not always the case - some children are able to resist the spirits that have afflicted their parents, but those who have little resistance are always adversely affected.

You need to realize that every problem you have is not caused by a familiar spirit, by a spirit that manifested itself in your family, or in one of your close associates. Some of your problems are caused by spirits who have just arrived on the scene. Evil spirits are like weeds in a garden, they get bigger and stronger with very little encouragement. They will become familiar with you quickly, and they will move right in and begin to dominate your life if you let them. When I realized that spirits were passed down from family member to family member, as if they were "inherited" so to speak, I was startled to see the same problems surfacing in related groups.

Like father, like son!

Children who have the same set of problems and afflictions that their parents have.

Double trouble!

CHAPTER SEVEN
SPIRITS ARE JUST SPIRITS!

Thank God Believers do not have to be fearful of these spirits. The purpose of this book is to show you how to recognize the spirits the devil has assigned to your case, and to instruct you on how to deal with them.

The Bible says in Ephesians 6:12,

"FOR WE WRESTLE NOT AGAINST FLESH AND BLOOD, BUT AGAINST PRINCIPALITIES, AGAINST POWERS, AGAINST THE RULERS OF THE DARKNESS OF THIS WORLD, AGAINST SPIRITUAL WICKEDNESS IN HIGH PLACES."

We are in a war, but if we never recognize our enemy, if we never take our basic training in the Word of God, then we will never be effective warriors here on earth. May I say that again?

"If we never recognize our enemy, if we never take our basic training in the Word of God, then we will never be effective warriors here on earth."

One day as I was driving to Akron, I was meditating on the Word of God and thinking about the different levels of spirits. I was wondering why some of them seemed to go easily, and why some of them were extremely stubborn. In the midst of my meditation, the Lord spoke to me and said, "Son, spirits are just spirits."

I thought about the Word from the Lord for awhile, and rolled it around in my spirit, and the Holy Spirit quickened to me that He was reminding me that all spirits,

> *"The long and the tall, the short and the small, the headache spirits as well as the cancer spirits, the arthritis spirits, and the quarrelsome spirits - all spirits are just spirits!"*

Every spirit, regardless of its name, or its rank, or its serial number is subject to the Precious Name of the Lord Jesus Christ.

Well, Praise God, I got happy, and I began to shout a little as I drove down the road, because I remembered what the Holy Spirit told Paul to tell us in Ephesians 1 starting with verse 17.

"THAT THE GOD OF OUR LORD JESUS CHRIST, THE FATHER OF GLORY, MAY GIVE TO YOU A SPIRIT OF WISDOM AND OF REVELATION IN THE KNOWLEDGE OF HIM. I PRAY THAT THE EYES OF YOUR HEART MAY BE ENLIGHTENED, SO THAT YOU MAY KNOW WHAT IS THE HOPE OF HIS CALLING, WHAT ARE THE RICHES OF THE GLORY OF HIS INHERITANCE IN THE SAINTS. AND WHAT IS THE SURPASSING GREAT-NESS OF HIS POWER TOWARD US WHO BELIEVE.

THESE ARE IN ACCORDANCE WITH THE WORKING OF THE STRENGTH OF HIS MIGHT WHICH HE BROUGHT ABOUT IN CHRIST, WHEN HE RAISED HIM FROM THE DEAD, AND SEATED HIM AT HIS RIGHT HAND IN THE HEAVENLY PLACES,
FAR ABOVE ALL RULE AND AUTHORITY AND POWER AND DOMINION, AND EVERY NAME THAT IS NAMED, NOT ONLY IN THIS AGE, BUT ALSO IN THE ONE TO COME.
AND HE PUT ALL THINGS IN SUBJECTION UNDER HIS FEET, AND GAVE HIM AS HEAD OVER ALL THINGS TO THE CHURCH, WHICH IS HIS BODY, THE FULLNESS OF HIM WHO FILLS ALL IN ALL."

Paul is praying for you and for me in this Chapter. Paul is praying that God will let us know who we are in Christ, and what the surpassing greatness of His Power is toward us who believe. Do you realize that the Holy Ghost is talking about us? About you and about me! Well, you are a Believer, aren't you? Sure you are, that is the way you got saved. You believed with your heart, and you confessed Jesus as Lord with your mouth.

Paul is telling us that God raised Christ from the dead and seated Him at His right hand in the Heavenly Places - far above - far - far - far above all rule and authority and power and every name that is named, not only in this age, but in the age to come. That He put all things in subjection under His feet, and gave Him as Head over ALL things to the Church which is His Body, and that's you and me.

We are the Body of Christ! You are a part of His Precious Body!

And as his Body, you are attached to the Head, and since the Head is far above all the Principalities and Powers, His Body is also far above them. Guess what you are far above, then? In Christ you are far above every single one of those old Familiar Spirits who have been messing around with you.

Where are you? Why far above them, of course. That is what the Bible says - they are under your feet! And now that you know this truth, it is perfectly all right for you to give them a little kick every now and then, because they have kicked you around for so long. You ought to be certain that you land a good kick or two on the "Inadequacy" and on the "It will never work for you" Spirits, because these spirits have especially enjoyed kicking you around and putting you down!

The Bible says you're a brand new creature in Christ Jesus in 2 Corinthians 5:17. And it is about time you started acting like the new creature you are, instead of nursing all those hang-ups that the devil has been hanging on your old creature for so long.

Spirits are just Spirits!

Take charge of them! Cast them out! Rebuke them! Command that they go! Name them by name, and send them on their way. You can do it, Jesus said you could!

In Mark 16:17 He said..."**IN MY NAME,** (In the same Name that is above every name that is named) **YOU SHALL CAST OUT DEMONS.**" Cast them out of your life and out of the lives of your loved ones. In Luke 10:17 the 70 came back rejoicing to Jesus, saying,

"LORD, EVEN THE DEMONS ARE SUBJECT TO US IN YOUR NAME."

Demons are subject to the Name of Jesus! Read it again if you are not sure about it. Jesus gave the Church the same authority in Mark 16; and since you are part of the Church, you have the right and the authority to cast demon spirits out of your life!

Until you do, they will continue to be familiar with you, and they will cause you the same set of problems that they have always caused -

Grief, strife, unhappiness, loneliness, inadequacy, sickness, poverty, bad, gloom. ...Do you remember the three stooges? Doubt! Despair! Doom!

Aren't you tired of these guys hanging around in your life? Well, let me tell you that they are going to stay there, right in the middle of your life, messing up your peace, your health and your happiness, until you take your place in the Body of Christ, and in His Name do some housecleaning!

It is about time you did some spiritual housecleaning, isn't it?

You do not have to wait for a particular season to clean your house. God's Word works the same in every life in every season - spring - summer - fall - winter. You can clean the spirits out of your life whenever you are ready. The Name of Jesus is always above the name of every spirit that is trying to defeat you - and faith in His Name will create a life of victory for you. So you can clean the spirits out of your life wherever you live! - Whether the sun is shining or whether there is snow on the ground.

If you want to make the Familiar Spirits in your life unfamiliar, you must change the way you are living. You must change the way you act and the way you react to situations, and you must put a muzzle on your mouth.

Many people are defeated in life by what they say. Their words defeat them. Is what you say really important? Well, you know what you say is important because Jesus told us in Matthew 12:37, **"FOR BY YOUR WORDS YOU SHALL BE JUSTIFIED, AND BY YOUR WORDS YOU SHALL BE CONDEMNED."** Your words encourage you or they will discourage you. And your words tell the devil everything he needs to know about you.

Look at another Scripture with me in Proverbs 18:20 about the importance of your words:

"WITH THE FRUIT OF A MAN'S MOUTH HIS STOMACH WILL BE SATISFIED; HE WILL BE SATISFIED WITH THE PRODUCT OF HIS LIPS."

Your mouth produces! All of us receive by agreeing with what is conveyed to us by thought or action or deed! We agree by acknowledging with our mouths and by our actions. For instance, you agree to a marriage proposal by accepting or proposing, and then by doing what is necessary to get married. You agree to purchasing your automobile by saying "Yes, that is the one I want," and then by meeting the requirements to take delivery of the car.

With the fruit of your mouth - your words - you will be satisfied because your words are productive. They will produce! They have always produced, and they will always produce. God made them that way - He said in Genesis 1:3 **"LET THERE BE LIGHT;"** and there was light. Your words bring light into your life or they bring darkness to you.

The next verse - Proverbs 18:21 declares, **"DEATH AND LIFE ARE IN THE POWER OF THE TONGUE..."** It is your tongue so you have the right to control it - you can tell your tongue what to do. If you are not sure what to tell it - let me give you one more instruction about your tongue that is recorded in Proverbs 12:18:

"...BUT THE TONGUE OF THE WISE BRINGS HEALING."

The Bible says your tongue can bring healing into your life or it can bring grief. Death or life! Train it to bring healing! Your tongue speaking God's Word, with the necessary corresponding actions in your life, can bring healing to your body, to your emotions, to your finances, to your marriage - to every area of your life. Your tongue determines in many respects the harvest you reap in this life.

Words are seeds sown in your life. You will reap a harvest of the seeds that you sow in you with your words, and the seeds that others sow in you with their words. You are the only one who can determine whether you will come rejoicing bringing in the sheaves at harvest time, or if you will come crying. You will come one way or the other because seeds sown will always be harvested!

There was a slogan in the Second World War that encouraged people - especially those who worked in the defense industry and in the ship yards - to be careful what they said about shipping schedules. The slogan was

"Loose Lips Sink Ships." That needs to be one of your slogans in your new walk with Christ - Do not let your loose lips sink your ship!

Let your tongue bring healing into your life!

SECTION II

CHAPTER EIGHT

INADEQUACY SPIRITS

The Familiar Spirits that I see manifested more than any other spirits as I minister, are the "Inadequacy Spirits."

The "I can't make it spirit!" The "I am not tall enough, I am not strong enough, I am not pretty enough, my breasts are not big enough, I do not know enough of God's Word, I have not fasted long enough, my teeth are not straight enough, my hair is not curly enough, I cannot jog far enough. - The I am not worthy spirit!"

These spirits manifest themselves in many ways, but their message is always the same!

You are not good enough and you are not going to get what you want in life. You are Inadequate! Inferior! And Unworthy!

Does that sound familiar to you? Has one of these spirits been hanging around you for so long that it has become familiar with you? I know it has become familiar with a bunch of people, because I deal with this spirit in almost every meeting. I see this spirit manifested most frequently in women. I am not suggesting that this spirit restricts its activities to females only, it also operates in the male species; but many men think they are too macho - they think they are too tough to admit that they have a problem, and as a result of their false pride they continue to struggle along with this spirit influencing and dominating much of their lives.

You need to recognize this Inadequacy Spirit for what it is. You need to realize that it comes straight from the pits of Hell, and then deal with it with the Word of God!

Lots of people spend so much time looking at, and pampering, and being controlled by their bodies - by their flesh - that they seem to have forgotten that the Bible says God looks at our hearts!

God spoke to Samuel in 1 Samuel 16:7, when He sent Samuel to Bethlehem to crown a new King, but the Lord did not tell Samuel which one of Jesse's sons to anoint as king. When Samuel got to Bethlehem he tried to anoint Eliab, the first born son, as King, because Samuel thought Eliab looked just like a King ought to look. He was tall, strong, striking; but God knew what Samuel was thinking; He knew his thoughts.

God does know your thoughts you know, and since you know that He knows your thoughts, that should give you the determination to straighten out your thinking. I have a friend, Charley Lane, who says, "One of the principle problems with the church is Stinking Thinking!" Most of the time I agree with him. If we would get our thinking in line with God's Word, we would think like God thinks, and then we would get on about His Business, instead of always concentrating on our own wants and desires.

God knew what Samuel was thinking and He said:

"...MAN LOOKS ON THE OUTWARD APPEARANCE, BUT THE LORD LOOKS AT THE HEART."

God looks at your heart! Man still looks at your outward appearance, just like God said, and it is your outward appearance - the "you" that you look at in the mirror - that the devil will use to your disadvantage! He will get you to concentrate on how you look on the outside - on your exterior - on the part of you whose destiny is dust - to convince you that you are not worthy, or good enough to receive from God.

One of the devil's favorite ways to get to you, is to tell you that you are not as smart, or as pretty, or as sophisticated as someone else - and then that guy will point out that specific someone to you to prove his point. He will show you someone prettier or smarter or more sophisticated than you are.

Now if you belong to the Lord you will be certain that you do look presentable on the outside, you will not be offensive, but you need to know that,

It is not how you look on the outside that counts, it is how you feel on the inside that makes you successful, or makes you want to give up and quit!

The devil doesn't care how pretty you are, or how you have fixed your hair, or how nice your perfume smells. He doesn't care how far you can jog; or how many push-ups you can do; or what your golf score is; or what your I.Q. level is. He doesn't even care how much money you have in the bank.

Now he will use all these carnal things to trap you if he can. He will try to get you so interested in your pretty face, or in your magnificent body, or in your affluent life-style, or in your retirement plan, or in your family, so you will not have time to find out what God's Word says. Because the devil knows that if you do not find out what God's Word says you will always be an easy target for him - and he will use you for target practice. The devil loves easy targets! Have you been one?

Beloved, be assured that the only thing that will defeat the devil in your life is what you do with the Word of God. Nothing more and nothing less!

If you were in one of my teaching sessions, I would repeat this line. May I? You need to realize that the only thing that will defeat the devil in your life is what you do with the Word of God - nothing more and nothing less.

TELEVISION COMPETITION

Most of us have grown up in the television era where sex, violence, liquor, and many of the other tools of the devil are prominently displayed. Let me exaggerate a little and tell you what the advertisements or the programs on TV seem to be saying.

"If you are not using our product or, smiling like I do, or feeling mighty fine with the whiskey and wine that I am drinking or selling, then there is something wrong with you. You just don't

understand living and the finer things in life, and certainly 'poor little old you out in hick town' (wherever that is), cannot make it unless you look and act like us."

These models and actresses always seem to be so pretty and so sophisticated.

Women seem to be the prime targets of this media blitz, whether it is in the form of advertisements or in the program content. Ladies, your competition comes smiling and dancing into your living room almost every day, and my, are they gorgeous! Do you know that the devil will do his best to convince you that you are not desirable unless you have a perfect smile, unless you walk with a tantalizing wiggle, and unless you have a bust size of 38 or so?

Isn't that the way those gals always look on TV or in the movies? The devil will tell you, that unless you are a carbon copy of these models, you are not going to make it! Thank God, that is not true! - I want to say that again - Thank God, that is not true!

The way you look does not have anything to do with how adequate you feel! External things do not necessarily have anything to do with adequacy, or with how you feel inside. Your adequacy is based on your relationship with the Lord - on what He did for you when you were saved - when you became a new creature in Christ. Adequacy does not depend on your smile or on your figure.

Let me share an example of adequacy with you that will demonstrate that outward appearance does not make you adequate. Do you remember Marilyn Monroe? She was a movie star and was proclaimed by many to be the "sexiest" woman in Hollywood and perhaps in the world. She was the ultimate sex symbol to many. But at the height of her career, some of the same old spirits who hang around you, were hanging around her: and, believe me, they were not telling her how gorgeous and beautiful she was. They were constantly feeding her the same line they keep loading you down with - Inadequacy!

> *"Marilyn, you are inadequate, and you are not going to make it. It doesn't make any difference how many movies you make or how many people tell you that you are gorgeous. You were born a loser, you have been a loser all of your life, and you are going to continue to be a loser! You are not worthy, and you are not going to make it!"*

This bunch kept talking to her, until finally she succumbed to their lies. The Liar lied to her so often that she became brainwashed, and she believed what the Deceiver said more than she believed what her public, her friends, and her publicity releases said. The medical reports declare that she committed suicide. She apparently didn't think she could make it!

She still felt the same way inside that she felt when she was a little girl....She had grown up; she had a beautiful smile, she walked with a wiggle, and she had a bust size of 38 or so, but she still felt inadequate! She had not changed inside, and when those old spirits kept insisting that she was a loser, she finally agreed with them. They convinced her that she could not make it, and she quit! She gave up and gave in to them!

Marilyn had a beautiful body, and a beautiful face - listen, she would be tough competition for most of the gals you see on TV who make you feel a little dowdy sometimes - but, inside she felt inadequate, and she didn't make it.

She had everything in the natural to live for, but the battle she was fighting was supernatural, and the only weapons she had were of the flesh. So, she lost the battle.

Carnal weapons do not count for much when you are fighting the devil.

Thank God, you are not limited to carnal weapons. Paul told us in 2 Corinthians 10:4, **"FOR THE WEAPONS OF OUR WARFARE ARE NOT CARNAL, BUT MIGHTY THROUGH GOD TO THE PULLING DOWN OF STRONGHOLDS."**

If you never realize that you are in a spiritual battle - And if you do not use the weapons God has provided for you - You are going to lose lots of battles in this life.

CHAPTER NINE

INADEQUACY SPIRITS WILL TRY TO MAKE YOU A LOSER

Do you know what makes people losers? Why it is how they feel inside. Sure it is. The Bible says in Proverbs 23:7,

"....AS A MAN THINKETH IN HIS HEART, SO IS HE."

As you think in your heart, so are you. Paul talks about your inner man, the person who lives in you throughout the Scriptures. It is how you feel inside that counts!

If a girl thinks she is a prostitute she will act like a prostitute. If a young man thinks he is a bum, he will act like a bum. If you think you are worthless, you will be worthless! As you think in your heart (in your inner man) so will you be.

Inadequacy - this spirit influences so many peoples' lives. This is the spirit that will try to make young women sleep around before they are married. These spirits will try to make them think that they have to sleep with a guy to be accepted - to belong - to get along.

What a lie of the devil! This same spirit encourages young men to take dope or drink, or steal a car. This spirit will say, or cause someone to say, "Come on -

everyone is doing it." Sometimes that is true -
sometimes everyone is "doing it" when the doing it is
bad! Maybe that is what they were saying in Sodom
and Gomorrah just before the fire fell - "Everyone is
doing it!" Maybe that is what they were saying in Rome
when their society crumbled. Maybe that is what they
are saying in Las Vegas, or in San Francisco. Maybe
that is even what they are saying in your town today!

"Come on, live a little, just relax and enjoy yourself,
everyone is doing it!"

The devil will try to convince you that it is easier to
do than to don't! But the Holy Spirit said "Don't" in
Romans 12:2, remember? He said, **"Don't be
conformed to this world, but be ye transformed..."**
The Holy Spirit said, **"Don't be conformed to evil! Be
transformed by the renewing of your mind so you
can receive from me!"**

*Inadequacy is not some new spirit that just
arrived on the scene.*

It was in operation long ago, ever since the devil
schemed his way into the Garden of Eden by deceiving
Eve, and then by seducing Adam to sin. Inadequacy's
favorite traveling companions are Fear and Anxiety and
Jealousy. And their specific job is to keep you from
receiving the things God has promised you in His
Word. That means they will try to keep you out of your
Promised Land. Let me show you some Biblical
examples of how they work.

Let's go to the third chapter of Exodus. When
Moses was a baby he was rescued from the Ark in the
Nile river by Pharaoh's daughter, and he was raised as
her son. When he was grown, he visited his brethren
where he saw an Egyptian beating a Hebrew slave, and

after he interceded and killed the Egyptian, he fled to Midian. Moses was 40 years old when he left Egypt, and now 40 years had passed in Midian. He had grown up with all the advantages of a Prince - as the son of Pharaoh's daughter he'd had the best of everything. The Bible says he was a man of power in word and in deeds.

He had not grown up in lack or in want or in poverty, and then when he got to Midian he had married Zipporah, the Priest of Midian's daughter. He had not been raised as a nobody and he was not a nobody now.

But when God spoke to him at the burning bush, in Exodus 3:4, and told him what He planned for him to do, Moses' reply in Exodus 3:11 was,

"WHO AM I, THAT I SHOULD GO TO PHARAOH?..."

Who am I? Isn't that the same nagging question that the devil always throws at you when you get ready to do anything positive? To do anything new? "Who are you to try to do this thing? You can't do that! It won't work for you!"

The Spirit of Inadequacy will manifest itself instantly. Remember, inadequacy is not a new spirit. It always operates the same way, and it will try to do it's thing on you just like it did on Moses. Let me show you how God dealt with Moses' feelings and with his profession of inadequacy. After some dialogue, God said in Exodus 3:14,

"I AM THAT I AM!" HE SAID, "THUS YOU SHALL SAY TO THE SONS OF ISRAEL, I AM HAS SENT ME TO YOU."

The Lord said, "I AM THAT I AM." My paraphrase is, God said, "I am all you need." I AM is current tense. God did not say, "It is what I used to be!" Nor did He say, "It is what I will be some day!" He said, "I AM all you need today!" He was saying, "Moses, I am not depending on your ability to set my children free, I am depending on My Ability in you to get the job done."

That is exactly what He is saying to you. He still is the same "I AM" that He was at the burning bush. God is not depending on your ability to do anything, He is depending on His Ability in you! When Moses was finally convinced that what God said was true, he acted on God's Word and led the Children of Israel out of bondage.

The Bible says in James 1:22,

"BUT BE YE DOERS OF THE WORD, AND NOT HEARERS ONLY..."

Moses became a "doer", and when he did what God told him to do, he changed his life-style. Would you like to change yours? You can!

Now this Spirit of Inadequacy didn't just lie down and quit when Moses overcame it with the Word of God. It kept right on trying to convince the Israelites that they were not adequate or worthy enough to receive the good things God had promised them.

The Children of Israel had been slaves all their lives and even after they had been delivered from the bondage of Egypt, they were fairly easy to convince that they were not worthy to occupy the Promised Land. The account of the twelve spies in Numbers 13 and 14 is a good example. The Israelites had been in the Wilderness for about a year or so by now, and the Lord spoke to Moses and told him to send a scouting party into the Promised Land; so Moses selected a leader from each of the twelve tribes, including Joshua and Caleb, and sent them to spy out the Land of Canaan.

Let's join them after they have spent 40 days in the Promised Land. The 12 have just returned from spying out the land, and now the 10 are giving their majority report to Moses and to the Congregation in Numbers 13:27-28, 31-33.

"...WE WENT INTO THE LAND WHERE YOU SENT US: AND IT CERTAINLY DOES FLOW WITH MILK AND HONEY, AND THIS IS ITS FRUIT." (and they showed them the large cluster of grapes)

"NEVERTHELESS, THE PEOPLE WHO LIVE IN THE LAND ARE STRONG, AND THE CITIES ARE FORTIFIED AND VERY LARGE; AND MOREOVER, WE SAW THE DESCENDANTS OF ANAK THERE..."

"BUT THE MEN WHO HAD GONE UP WITH CALEB AND JOSHUA SAID, 'WE ARE NOT ABLE TO GO UP AGAINST THE PEOPLE, FOR THEY ARE TOO STRONG FOR US.' SO THEY GAVE OUT TO THE SONS OF ISRAEL AN EVIL REPORT OF THE LAND WHICH THEY HAD SPIED OUT, SAYING, 'THE LAND THROUGH WHICH WE HAVE GONE, IN SPYING IT OUT, IS A LAND THAT DEVOURS ITS INHABITANTS: AND ALL THE PEOPLE WHOM WE SAW IN IT ARE MEN OF GREAT SIZE.

THERE ALSO WE SAW THE NEPHILIM (THE SONS OF ANAK ARE PART OF THE NEPHILIM); AND WE BECAME LIKE GRASSHOPPERS IN OUR OWN SIGHT,

AND SO WE WERE IN THEIR SIGHT!' "

To understand the full impact of this negative report, you need to read Numbers 13 and 14, and realize what the Lord was trying to do for His Children. He wanted to give them the Land He had promised to give to their Fathers, to Abraham, to Isaac, and to Jacob so He sent them to inspect the Land and when they came back they reported to Moses:

The land is good, it is just like God said it would be! It is flowing with milk and honey, and its fruit is so big that it takes two men to carry one cluster of grapes. We've never seen anything as good as this, **but nevertheless,** *regardless of all this good stuff, regardless of the fact that everything that God told us about the land is true, the people who are living in our Promised Land are giants. They are so big that we became like grasshoppers in our own sight, and I know that's how we looked to them.*

I call this the "Grasshopper Theology" syndrome. The "But, Nevertheless" religion!

What is the "But, Nevertheless" religion? It is when you say, "I know what God's Word says, but nevertheless it does not work for me."

"I know God's Word says that by Jesus' stripes I was healed, but nevertheless I hurt so I must be sick."

"I know God's Word says "Give and it shall be given unto you...', but nevertheless I don't tithe and I don't give because my money is my money and I just have enough for me."

"I know God's Word says Forgive, but you really do not understand what they did to me." And it goes on and on...I know what God's Word says, "But, Nevertheless!"

The Grasshopper Theology syndrome is always manifested when we insist on walking by our sense nature when our senses contradict God's Word. I call this the "Goat" religion, because there is a but after every one of God's Promises.

If you practice this theology - if you but nevertheless too much - you will "Butt" yourself out of The Promised Land.

CIRCUMSTANTIAL EVIDENCE

The old Inadequacy Spirit had shown up in Numbers 13 and 14 again. Caleb and Joshua knew that God's Word would prevail over every circumstance, but the circumstantial evidence in this case came in the form of a bunch of giants, and the other ten believed what they could see with their eyes more than they believed God's Word. They brought an evil report to the Children of Israel, and the Israelites believed the

Majority report. Do you remember what happened?
Hebrews 3:19 says:

**"...THEY WERE NOT ABLE TO ENTER
BECAUSE OF UNBELIEF."**

The Spirits of Inadequacy and Doubt and Unbelief,
kept the Children of Israel from entering into their
Promised Land. The devil convinced them that they
were not big enough, or worthy enough, or strong
enough to possess the Land that God had promised
them, and as a result of their unbelief, they never
possessed God's Promises in their lives. And the Bible
says they were so disappointed and unhappy about
their lot in life that they cried the whole night through.
That's what Numbers 14:1 says:

**"AND ALL THE CONGREGATION LIFTED UP
THEIR VOICE, AND CRIED AND THE PEOPLE
WEPT THAT NIGHT."**

That's right! It will happen every time. When you
rely on man's word when it contradicts God's Word,
you are going to shed lots of tears. You will cry all
night long! Has it ever happened to you?

Do you know that all of those who believed the
majority report, every single one of them perished in
the Wilderness? The ones God promised the Promised
Land to, were not able to enter into the land He had
promised them because they did not believe what God
said. Their unbelief kept them living in the Wilderness!
What will yours do to you?

Why does the Bible say that the ten brought an evil
report in Numbers 13:32? They were only reporting the
facts as they saw them, weren't they? The Bible says

they brought an evil report because they said, "We cannot do what God said we could do." By their report they took sides against God's Word, and that is evil.

You are a reporter too, you know; sure you are - you bring a good report, or you bring a bad report, on every area of your life. Since you know now that you can bring an evil report, you need to be certain that you are on the God-Side of every issue. The God-Side of every issue is what God's Word says, not what your senses tell you.

These Spirits will try to do the very same thing to you. They will try to lay this "Grasshopper Theology" complex or the "But, Nevertheless" religion on you if you will let them. Thank God you know better, don't you? Sure you do.

One more example!

Turn with me to the Book of Judges. The Children of Israel finally got out of the Wilderness; they have crossed the river Jordan, and now they have partially occupied the Promised Land. Joshua and Caleb, and Deborah and Barak have all gone on to Abraham's Bosom, and now the Children of Israel were in trouble again because they were not honoring God's Word. Judges 6:1 says:

"THEN THE SONS OF ISRAEL DID WHAT WAS EVIL IN THE SIGHT OF THE LORD; AND THE LORD GAVE THEM INTO THE HANDS OF MIDIAN SEVEN YEARS."

They were living in the Promised Land all right, but they were not enjoying any of its benefits. Does that sound familiar? Surely that is not happening in your life, is it?

In this chapter the Children of Israel were hiding from the enemy in caves because they were afraid. They were not doing and keeping God's Word and because of their disobedience, their enemies ruled over them. Then the Angel of the Lord appeared to Gideon to tell him how to defeat the enemy, and in verse 14-15, the angel said:

"GO IN THIS YOUR STRENGTH AND DELIVER ISRAEL FROM THE HAND OF MIDIAN. HAVE I NOT SENT YOU?"
AND GIDEON REPLIED TO HIM, "O LORD, HOW SHALL I DELIVER ISRAEL? BEHOLD, MY FAMILY IS THE LEAST IN MANASSEH, AND I AM THE YOUNGEST IN MY FATHER'S HOUSE."

Do you understand Gideon's reply to the Angel of the Lord? The Spirit of Inadequacy had moved right in with him - That spirit was living with Gideon down in the wine press where he was hiding from the enemy, and this spirit had convinced Gideon that his only possible answer was:

"I am not big enough! I am not strong enough! My family is not worthy, and even if they were - I am not worthy because I am the least one of the whole bunch!"

Now Gideon was pretty sure he was not tough enough to whip the Midianites, because he'd had some first hand experience with them - and they had beaten him every time. That is the reason he was hiding from them in the wine press. As a result of his previous defeats - as a result of his experiences - the devil had stolen all of God's Promises from him, and now he had to hide from the enemy to thrash his wheat. He was hiding because they would steal his harvest from him if he thrashed his wheat in the open.

The devil is still just the same. Jesus has not changed and the devil hasn't changed. He operates the same way he always did - he will try to convince you that you never will be happy, and successful, and satisfied. Your enemy will always look like a huge giant! These spirits always look like they are too tough for you to handle. Problems always look like they are giants, don't they? The devil knows that if he sent a bunch of dwarfs to harass you, you wouldn't pay any attention to them. You would just kick them out of your way and get on about your business. Problems are not really giants, anyway; they just look like giants to your natural eyes. When you begin to look at them through eyes of faith, God's Word always shrinks them down to their proper size! - The mountains become molehills! - Insignificant!

Thank God Gideon finally believed the Lord, and he climbed out of the pit he was hiding in, and he did exactly what God told him to do - whether he felt like he could do it or not. Then when Gideon did what God told him to do, God did what He said He would do - He delivered Israel!

Did you note that in two out of the three cases that we have looked at, that when God's people acted on His Word, God's Word came to pass? Moses acted, and Gideon acted, and when they did, God acted. God did exactly what He said He would do. Neither of these men felt like they could do what God told them to do, but "acting in faith," they became "doers of the Word and not hearers only," and when they "acted" God gave them the victory He had promised them.

You need to pay particular attention to the other example. The facts are that when the majority refused to act on God's Word, they never did enjoy the Promises of God in their lives. 600,000 men thought they were right, but they were wrong! Do you realize that #'s do not mean a single thing when you are wrong. This whole bunch died in the Wilderness! Do you know that it still works exactly the same way today - you can act on God's Word, or you can refuse to act.

You can believe, or you can believe not. If you are not obedient to God's Word, you cannot defeat the devil in your life.

The same spirits of inadequacy and unbelief will try to keep you out of your Promised Land just like they kept the Children of Israel out of their Promised Land. Remember - God is just the same! God does not change, and neither does the devil. The Bible was written for your benefit. God wrote the Bible so it would be profitable to you. The Bible was written so you can see how men and women of God were obedient to God's Word and defeated the enemy in their lives. The wonderful thing is, when you apply these same principles in your life, you too will enjoy the Promises God made to you in His Word.

Promised Land Instructions, that is how one of the sub-titles of the Bible might read, because God gives us instructions in His Word on how we can dwell in the land of Milk and Honey that He has promised to us.

In 2 Corinthians 1:20 the Holy Spirit said,

"FOR ALL THE PROMISES OF GOD IN HIM, ARE YEA, AND IN HIM AMEN, UNTO THE GLORY OF GOD BY US."

God gets glory out of His Children enjoying His Promises in their lives. He made His promises to you, and His Promises are for you. God does not get any glory out of you being an Inadequate, Defeated, Poverty-stricken, Unworthy, Christian. He recorded His Word for us. The Bible says in Galatians 5:1:

"IT WAS FOR FREEDOM THAT CHRIST SET US FREE....."

Jesus set you free so you could enjoy His freedom! You have the right to live in the freedom that Christ provided for you in every area of your life. You can change your address from 301 Inadequate Avenue to # 1 Promised Land Lane if you study and learn how to apply His Word to you.

CHAPTER TEN

JESUS CHRIST IS JUST THE SAME!

The Bible says in Hebrews 13:8,

"JESUS CHRIST IS THE SAME, YESTERDAY, TODAY, AND FOREVER."

Jesus has not changed! Jesus is still concerned about you, and He is still concerned about the whole world. Since Jesus is still the same, do you know this means that he still feels the same about sin? Sin is still sin! Sin is not a casual thing to God. God was so concerned about sin that He sent His only begotten Son to deal with sin - Jesus made the perfect and final atonement for sin at Calvary! Jesus came so we could be set free from sin. He did not come so we could continue to be overcome by the sinful nature of the flesh and of the world. He came so we could live victoriously in Him. Remember where the promises of God are? They are in Him!

And then the Bible tells us in 1 John 3:8:

"...THE SON OF GOD APPEARED FOR THIS PURPOSE, THAT HE MIGHT DESTROY THE WORKS OF THE DEVIL!"

That is why Jesus came, to destroy the works of the devil. Do you think that might include the works the devil has been working in your life? Well, of course it does. Praise God! Doesn't that make you happy! Aren't you happy that Jesus came to set you free, that you don't have to go around with a long face or with a long inside saying, "Oh woe is me, how am I ever going to make it?" You need to recognize that your enemy is still the devil, and then you need to learn enough of God's Word to establish your place in His Kingdom. Jesus expects you to be something special, because you are something special. He has high hopes for you, why He told you in Matthew 5:48:

"THEREFORE YOU ARE TO BE PERFECT, AS YOUR HEAVENLY FATHER IS PERFECT."

Does that sound as if Jesus has given up on you? Does that sound as if He thinks you are inadequate? That you are a loser? That you are not worthy? Of course not; you have been bought with a price, and the Bible says your body is the Temple of the Holy Ghost. God's Temple is full of His anointing, and it is God's Anointing that breaks the yoke of bondage in every Believers' life. The anointing that breaks the yoke dwells in you! Isn't that tremendous!

Do you remember what Jesus said about the devil in John 8:44? Just in case you have forgotten, let me read it to you.

"...HE WAS A MURDERER FROM THE BEGINNING, AND DOES NOT STAND IN THE TRUTH, BECAUSE THERE IS NO TRUTH IN HIM, WHENEVER HE SPEAKS A LIE, HE SPEAKS FROM HIS OWN NATURE; FOR HE IS A LIAR AND THE FATHER OF LIES."

Jesus said, "The devil is a liar!" Well, that is what He said, read it in your Bible. Now since you know that, since you know that the devil is a liar, why don't you begin to treat him like a liar? Why do you just keep listening to his lies? When he begins to try to unload that same old junk on you that he has been dumping on you most of your life -

Telling you that you are nothing, that you are not going to make it, that no one cares - that it does not make any difference - that God has forgotten your name and address, and that He never even knew your phone number -

do you know what you ought to do? Why, you ought to make him (the devil, the deceiver, the one who is constantly accusing you) listen to some of the promises God made to you in His Word instead of listening to his lies all the time! Do you know any promises? May I share a few good ones with you?

1. In John 15:16 Jesus said, **"YOU DID NOT CHOOSE ME BUT I CHOSE YOU AND ORDAINED YOU..."**

You did not get saved by accident. The wonderful part is - Jesus personally chose you for Himself.

2. Then in Ephesians 1:4 the Holy Ghost told Paul to tell you that, **"CHRIST CHOSE YOU IN HIM BEFORE THE FOUNDATION OF THE WORLD..."**

You are so special that long before you ever
existed in the flesh, Christ chose you in Him.
Hallelujah!

Now, you do not think Christ chose you for bad, do
you?
Did you ever choose up sides when you were a kid
to do anything: to play ball, or to play charades, or to
play a game of some sort? Did you ever choose
anyone for bad? Did you want them on your side so
they could lose? Well, of course you didn't. You
always wanted the losers on the other side, didn't you?
Well, the Lord did not choose you for bad either -
He chose you for good! If you, being evil, know how
to do good for your own, don't you think that the Lord
of Glory will do good for His Children? Of course, He
will.
God chose you for good! Say that with me, "God
chose me for good!"
Jesus did not save you and then just leave you here
all by yourself to struggle through. He did not fly off to
Heaven to float along on a cloud listening to the angels
play on their harps, and just hope that you would make
it to the Rapture. He has a tremendous plan for your
life, and He has recorded all of the details of His Plan
in the Bible. Do you know that it is the only Book He
ever wrote - and that it is a best seller. And do you also
know that He wrote a special part in the Bible just for
you? Do you know that you will never know what your
part is in His plan if you never read His Word. Do you
know what He said to you in His Book? He said in

3. Philippians 4:6-7 "BE ANXIOUS FOR
   NOTHING (don't worry about anything),

**BUT IN EVERYTHING BY PRAYER AND
SUPPLICATION, WITH THANKSGIVING, LET
YOUR REQUEST BE MADE KNOWN TO
GOD. AND THE PEACE OF GOD, WHICH
SURPASSES ALL COMPREHENSION,
SHALL GUARD YOUR HEARTS AND YOUR
MINDS IN CHRIST JESUS."**

Is that promise good enough for you?

If you had to select a promise, would this one be your choice - that you do not have to worry about anything? It is a good one isn't it! Did you notice when you were going to have the peace of God in your life? Why, it is when you stop worrying and stop being anxious - it is when you make your specific requests known to God by prayer and Supplication with Thanksgiving. You might as well turn your worries and problems over to God anyway, because you have not done too well with them, have you?

**"AND THE PEACE OF GOD WHICH
SURPASSES ALL COMPREHENSION, SHALL
GUARD YOUR HEARTS AND YOUR MINDS IN
CHRIST JESUS."**

God's peace has a job to do - its job is to guard your hearts (your inner man) and your minds (the thing you think and imagine with). God's peace is on guard in your life and it is about time that you learned how to relax and enjoy His security system.

Then He told Peter to tell you in 1 Peter 5:7,

**"CASTING ALL YOUR ANXIETY (CARE) UPON
HIM, BECAUSE HE CARES FOR YOU."**

When the Accuser of the Brethren, when the guy who accuses you of being a failure tells you that no one cares, and that your life does not matter - when he begins to tell you that you are nothing, a zero, a minus; when he begins to chant his incantations to you, lay that one on him!

You can say "Devil, God cares for me, and since I know that He cares for me, I do not care what you say anymore."

That will make him nervous, and then he will begin to squirm a little. He always gets anxious when God's Children start learning the Word, and Philippians 4:6 will not work for the devil. You have the right to let the Word become flesh in your life, and you have the right to live victoriously in Christ.

You can have your druthers you know.

You can cast all your cares - all your anxieties - on the Lord or you can keep them. It is up to you.

Do you know what druthers are? When I was a kid in Oklahoma, I'd druther do almost anything than weed the garden. Why, I'd druther go swimming, or fishing, I'd druther go noodling in the creek, or crack black walnuts, or just lie around in the sun.

My least favorite things in the world were to work in the garden or to eat liver. God gives us our druthers, and sometimes it seems like we'd druther cry and feel sorry for ourselves and agree with the lies of the Liar, rather than to believe God's Word. God gives us our druthers! Are you enjoying yours, or are you murmuring and complaining about them?

YOU CAN DO ALL THINGS

4. In Philippians 4:13 Paul said, **"I CAN DO ALL THINGS THROUGH CHRIST WHO STRENGTHENS ME."**

The Bible says God is not a respecter of persons. That means that God's Promises are applicable to all of us. "So what?" the devil may be telling you. The so what is that if Paul could do all things through Christ, then you, by applying God's Word to your specific situation, can also do all, ALL, not some things or part things, but all things through Christ, because Christ is the One who is strengthening you. The Bible does not say you can do all things by yourself, it says "THROUGH CHRIST." By staying in Him - "by abiding in the vine." Do you ever sing that song, "I'm abiding in the vine, abiding in the vine..." The text is from the 15th Chapter of John and the 7th verse reads,

"IF YOU ABIDE IN ME, AND MY WORDS ABIDE IN YOU, ASK WHATEVER YOU WISH, AND IT SHALL BE DONE FOR YOU."

No wonder you and Paul can do all things. It is because you are abiding in Christ and His Words are abiding in you. You are an abider, and Vine abiders are always winners!

Is being in the winner's circle a new category for you? Do you like it?

5. 2 Corinthians 2:14 **"BUT THANKS BE TO GOD, WHO ALWAYS** (Always, always,

always, always, does always really mean
always?) **CAUSES US TO TRIUMPH IN
CHRIST..."**

How often is God going to cause you to triumph in
Christ Jesus? Just on Sundays, maybe once or twice
in a blue moon? Is it just when you have cried for 13
years or so? Is it when you hold your face a certain
way? Of course not, the Bible says it is always! I can
almost hear some of you saying, "But I am not
triumphing always"...Well, whose fault is it, yours or
God's? Examine your life. Have you done what the
Bible says to do? Why you know you haven't, because
if you do what the Bible says to do - If you abide in
Christ and if His Words abide in you - You will triumph!
When you learn how to conduct Spiritual Warfare
according to God's instructions, you will win every
time.

The Bible is the Word of God, and in John 17:17
Jesus said,

**"SANCTIFY THEM IN THE TRUTH: THY WORD
IS TRUTH."**

The Word of God is the Truth, and the truth is that
God always causes you to triumph in Christ Jesus. So
if you are not triumphing, you need to get in Christ
Jesus! Do you think it is worth the effort...to triumph
always! Of course it is.

6. 2 Corinthians 5:21 **"HE MADE HIM WHO
    KNEW NO SIN TO BE SIN ON OUR
    BEHALF, THAT WE MIGHT BECOME
    THE RIGHTEOUSNESS OF GOD IN HIM."**

That means you have the right to become the Righteousness of God in Christ Jesus. You have His righteousness! Jesus is your righteousness! Don't let the devil ever tell you that you are not worthy again, because the Bible says, Jesus Christ bestowed His Righteousness on you when you received Him as Savior.

You are the Righteousness of God in Christ Jesus!

In the vernacular of today that means, "You are in good with God!" Is that all right?

Have you ever been in good with anyone before? A teacher maybe? If you were, do you remember that when you were in good with a particular teacher, it was easier for you to get along and to do good in that class. Do you know why? It is because you knew you were liked, and you knew that the one who was in control wanted good for you.

Were you ever in good with your boss - or have you ever known anyone who was? Whether it was you or someone else, being in good with the boss certainly made the job easier, didn't it? Well, I like being in good too, and I especially like being in good with my wife because when I am she makes a special effort to please me with her cooking. Sometimes she fixes fried chicken and fried okra for me. Don't laugh, if you are from Oklahoma, food does not come much better than that.

But let's get back to the point - do you know that since you are in good with God that He wants good for you, and He will do special things in your life. You are in good with God because of Jesus - and because of Jesus - God is for you! Aren't people you are in good with for you? Sure they are, and since you are the righteousness of God in Christ Jesus - that means God is for you! Do you know why that is so important? It is important because the Bible says in

7. Romans 8:31 "...IF GOD BE FOR US, WHO CAN BE AGAINST US?"

The Holy Ghost said, "Paul, I want you to tell my children, that I am for them, and since I am for them it does not make any difference who is against them because:

"I am the King of Kings and the Lord of Lords, I Am the I Am, I Am the Holy One of Israel, the Alpha and the Omega, the Beginning and the End, the First and the Last, the Creator!"

"I am the one who chose them in me before the foundation of the world, and I chose them for Good, and since I am for them the only one who can be against them is the devil, and he is subject to me in my children!" "That is why I came in the flesh, to destroy the works of the devil!"

"So I want each one of my children to keep on keeping on in me, to keep on abiding in the vine, so we can get on with my game plan for them!"

God's plan for you is good. He is for you! The Lord made you a winner. God has not chosen a loser yet, and He is not about to start with you.

You are not a loser!

Can't you just shout a little when you begin to see what God has in mind for you? I can. You ought to try it just one time, you might like it. I guarantee you that when you begin to quote some of God's promises to the devil, when you begin to resist him with the Word of God, that he will tuck his tail and flee. Remember what James told us in James 4:7-8:

"SUBMIT YOURSELVES THEREFORE TO GOD, RESIST (resist, resist, resist) THE DEVIL AND HE WILL FLEE FROM YOU.

DRAW NIGH TO GOD, AND HE WILL DRAW NIGH TO YOU."

You submit yourself to God by learning and by doing His Word, and then - and only then - you will have God's Power and His Authority to resist the devil. You cannot resist the devil if you do not submit yourself to God! Stop trying to resist the devil without submitting yourself to God, because it will not work. And don't just lie down and whimper,

"I don't know if the Bible is true or not."

Resist the devil with the Word of God. The Word of God is the sword of the Spirit, so learn how to use it! Do not quote the "begats" to the devil, tell him who you are in Christ - and remind him that you are in a fixed fight because Jesus fixed it for you in the end! He did, didn't He!

YOU ARE A NEW CREATURE IN CHRIST!

Let me share one other Scripture with you about adequacy. You know that your adequacy is the Lord. You are the Righteousness of God in Christ Jesus. You are in Christ because the Bible says in

8. 2 Corinthians 5:17 "...IF ANY MAN BE IN CHRIST, HE IS A NEW CREATURE..."

So that is what you are, a new creature in Christ.
Well, what is a new creature?
When you were born again, when you received the Lord Jesus Christ as Saviour, did the color of your eyes change? Did you become taller or shorter, fatter or skinnier? Better looking maybe? Maybe you are good looking enough already.
What does that mean "You are a new creature?" Well, it means that there is a new you in you. When you received Christ as your Saviour, He came to live in you. That's what the Bible says in John 14:23:

JESUS SAID, "IF YOU LOVE ME YOU WILL KEEP MY WORDS, AND MY FATHER WILL LOVE YOU, AND MY FATHER AND I WILL COME AND MAKE OUR ABODE WITH YOU."

How about that for special house guests! Do you think you should put a notice in the paper? "My house guests since I got saved are The Father and The Son, who have taken up permanent residence in me because I keep God's Commandments." The Father and the Son are living in you! Your spirit was born again. There is a new you in you, and as you feed that new creature (spirit) in you with the Word of God, He is going to grow up. Your inner man will mature and the new you in you will change the old you that you walk around in.

Why is that important?

It is important because people do not change how they feel inside unless they have some help from the Lord.

If you never realize who you are in Christ, all the old things that harassed and bothered you before you were saved, will continue to try to do their thing in you, if you allow them.

But, listen to me, since you are a new you, since you are in Christ Jesus, since you are abiding in the Vine, do you realize that the things that bothered the old you:

The problems, the weaknesses, the sicknesses, the loneliness, the habits, the fears, and the inadequacies,

do not have any right to hang around the new you? Of course they don't! If they do, they are trespassers, and you can cast them out of your life! They do not have any right to mess around in your life anymore,

Because you are a brand new creature in Christ.

And new creatures, new species do not have old creature problems. Praise God, it is the Truth. You are not an old patched up you, you are a brand new you, and the One living in you chose you to be a winner!

Since you are a new creature - since Jesus made you a winner - why do you still feel so inadequate sometime?

"How do I overcome inadequacy?" That is the question I hear frequently. Let me tell you how Paul handled inadequacy. Do you realize that Paul is the person that the Holy Spirit used to write seven of the eight points on adequacy that we have covered so far in this Chapter? Do you know why the Lord caused him to write so much about adequacy? Because Paul found the source of adequacy!

How did the man who the Lord used to write approximately one half of the New Testament feel about his own self sufficiency? Paul did not keep it a secret - he tells us very clearly how he felt in II Corinthians 3:5:

"NOT THAT WE ARE ADEQUATE IN OURSELVES TO CONSIDER ANYTHING AS COMING FROM OURSELVES, BUT OUR ADEQUACY IS FROM GOD."

Paul was not sufficient or adequate in himself - he learned how to depend on God, and so can you! As one of the Lord's new creations - you can learn to depend on God. You can do the same thing Paul did - you can let the adequacy of God be manifested in you.

VERILY, VERILY!

Look at John 14:12 with me.

"TRULY, TRULY, (KJ Translation reads Verily, Verily) I SAY TO YOU, HE WHO BELIEVES IN ME, THE WORKS THAT I DO SHALL HE DO ALSO; AND GREATER WORKS THAN THESE SHALL HE DO: BECAUSE I GO TO MY FATHER."

Isn't that a remarkable Scripture? Not only the works that He did, the Lord said, but greater works than these. Now most people skip over this Scripture, and the Scriptures like John 15:7, the Abiding Scripture. Have you ever noticed that? Most Christians skim right by the Power Scriptures, the Scriptures that require them to do something. The Scriptures that require them to believe and to act, and to be doers of the Word and not just hearers only. The Scriptures that instruct them to give unto the Gospel, to tithe, to fast, to put off the old man and to put on Christ - the Scriptures that instruct them to pray for more than 10 or 15 minutes at a time.

Does it bug you just a little sometimes when you find out that Jesus has put the responsibility for how you live on you?

He has, you know. If you never accept the responsibility of learning God's Word, and acting on it, the devil will always be hanging around your house, running in and out of your life through the revolving door you have installed for him.

Do you know that you give the devil unlimited access to you, and to yours by refusing to learn and to act on God's Word? And then because of your lack of knowledge he will beat you just like a drum. Is that a pretty picture?

I am from Oklahoma, and one of the things I enjoy doing is going to Indian Pow Wows. Well, at these Pow Wows, the Indians dress up in their native dress and they dance and they sing, and they play the drums - man, do they ever play those drums! They play them night and day, day in and day out; as long as the Pow Wow lasts, the drums are pounding.

Bom - bom - bom - bom - bom - bom -- dum - dum - dum - dum - dum - dum - dum - dum - dum - dum - dum - dum - dum - dum - the drums go on and on and on-

Do you realize that the devil will beat on you the same way the Indians beat on their drums until you learn your rights in Christ. And the good part is - when you learn your rights in Christ you can close down the devil's pow wow in your life. You remember how his drums sound - -

Dum-dum-dum-dumb-dumb-dumb-dumb! Yes, I said dumb!

The devil will continue to beat you all day, every day, if you will allow him. But Jesus gave us a remedy,

"IF YOU ABIDE IN ME AND MY WORDS ABIDE IN YOU, YOU SHALL ASK WHAT YOU WILL, AND IT SHALL BE DONE UNTO YOU."

"...IF MY WORDS ABIDE IN YOU..." In you - in you. It is entirely up to you! You can allow God's Word to abide in you, and when you do, you have the authority to ask what you will. Of course you will have to make an effort! But it is worth whatever you need to do to receive unlimited asking privileges!

Is the Bible science fiction? Is the Bible just a collection of stories that someone made up? If you are sure that it is not, then why are you treating it like it is a novel? Why don't you pay attention to it? Why don't you read it, why don't you study it? Why don't you meditate on it? Why don't you practice it? Why aren't you a doer of His Word instead of a hearer only?

Do you think that the Holy Ghost put these powerful Promise Scriptures in His "best-seller" to tantalize you, like dangling a carrot in front of a donkey, to get him to move? Why, of course He did not. He wrote the Bible for you and for me, so we could have life and have life more abundantly. He did not desert you, He has not forgotten your name and address. Jesus came to make his abode in you, remember? He is living in you...and the One living in you said,

"VERILY, VERILY, I SAY UNTO YOU, HE THAT BELIEVETH ON ME, THE WORKS THAT I DO SHALL HE DO ALSO: AND GREATER WORKS THAN THESE SHALL HE DO: BECAUSE I GO UNTO MY FATHER."

That is what Jesus said; can you believe it? Of course you can, because you are a Believer, aren't you? "..He that believeth on me ..." How can you do it? How can you ever do the Works Jesus did? Maybe the devil is whispering to you, "You can't even get your own life together, so how can you do the works Jesus did?"

The devil is still trying to work on you, isn't he? You ought to rejoice a little since you are beginning to recognize his tactics.

CHAPTER ELEVEN

DOES JESUS KNOW HOW YOU FEEL?

Does Jesus know how you feel inside? Have you fooled Him? Does the One who created you, the One who chose you in Him before the foundation of the World, think that you feel like you can do the things He did, or greater things, yet?

When I hear anyone quoting John 14:12, it is always in a humble, depreciating way, and they almost always say, "Why, how could I ever do greater things than the Lord?" What you and I need to do is to concentrate on doing the things that He did first, then we can move on to the greater things. Let's start doing the things the Lord did first. First things always come first! He said He came to Preach the Gospel - To bind up the broken hearted - To open the prison doors and to set the captives free! He came to proclaim the acceptable year of the Lord! The acceptable year of the Lord is the Year of Jubilee when everything is restored and everyone is set free! Jesus came to set us free!

We need to get on about the Lord's business instead of always majoring on how we feel, or on how we look. The devil can always keep us from doing the works that Jesus did if he can get us to concentrate on our inadequacies and inabilities, instead of concentrating on Jesus.

God does have a business, you know. Do you remember when Jesus was 12, and He and His parents went to Jerusalem to celebrate the Passover? His parents started back home without him and they did not miss him till evening. (This account is recorded in Luke 2.) Finally after looking for Him for three days, they found Him in the Temple both asking and answering questions. When Mary began to scold Him, He said:

"DID YOU NOT KNOW THAT I MUST BE ABOUT MY FATHER'S BUSINESS?"

God has a business. His business with Jesus at that time was for Him to grow up - to learn and to act on His Father's Word.

Has God changed His business?

In Malachi 3:6, God said

"...I AM THE LORD, AND I CHANGE NOT..."

God has not changed! He does not have a new business. God is not dead! He has not had a Going Out of Business Sale! He is not bankrupt! He is still the same! He is just like He always was, and His business with you is for you to learn His Word, and to grow up in the Lord so He can use you!

Your business is to learn who and what you are in Christ so you can get on about your Father's business! You will be about your Father's business when you are proclaiming the acceptable year of the Lord - when you are setting the captives free - and the first captive you need to set free is you!

Don't you know that Jesus knows how you feel inside?

Is it some secret that you have kept from him? Jesus knows, He knows everything about you including your thoughts. He knows that you do not feel like you can do the things He did. He even knows that you feel like you can not make it sometimes! He knows that the devil has been telling you that you are a loser for so long that sometimes you almost forget that you are on the winning team.

I think that one of the major problems with the Church is that it has amnesia! The Church has forgotten who it is and what its rights are in Christ Jesus! It has forgotten the promises of God! It is easy to remember the lies of the devil because that is what most people have listened to most of their lives while they were walking by their sense nature.

If we are going to insist on having amnesia, the best thing we can do is to get our amnesia straightened out and get it working right. What do I mean by that? I mean we need to get amnesia about the devil's lies and remember God's Promises. Maybe I will start a repair shop and call it an "Amnesia Straightener Outer Center." Could I count on you as one of my first customers?

Let me tell you something:

Jesus is not depending on your ability or on your adequacy to get the job done!

He is not depending on how you feel to do the works that He did. He is depending on His adequacy in you! He is depending on His ability in you! He is the One who came to live in you, isn't He? Don't you realize that He knows exactly how you feel on the inside and on the outside all the time? He knows that sometimes you feel so spiritually low that you need a stepladder to get your chin up to the curb.

But He is not depending on your adequacy, He is depending on His adequacy in you to do the works that He did, because no one can do those works except the Lord. He is living in you, He has made His abode in you, He has taken up His residence in you; and Praise God, it is Jesus in you who is going to do the same works He did when He walked on the Sea of Galilee!

When He healed the sick - when He raised the dead - when He fed the multitudes - and when He set the captives free! Jesus is just the same yesterday, today, and forever! He has not changed, and He will do the same things in you that He always did. He is in control of every situation.

Nothing is too hard, or too big or so desperate, or so impossible, that Jesus cannot handle it; it makes no difference whether it is sin, sickness, grief, loneliness, inadequacy, poverty, or any other spirit from the devil. They are all subject to the Name of Jesus!

Jesus is Lord of all, and since the Lord of all is in you, that means that wherever you are God is, and you and God are always a majority. Sure you are - with the Lord living in you you have the power to be in control of every situation.

"AND GREATER WORKS THAN THESE SHALL YOU DO BECAUSE I GO TO MY FATHER..."

How is that ever going to be? How will you ever do greater Works than Jesus? Listen, what did He say He would do when He went to His Father? Why, He said He would send the Holy Spirit, the Comforter. The one who was in the world, but the world could not see Him because they did not believe, and then He said that this Holy Spirit was going to dwell in us. Jesus said the Holy Spirit could not come in an indwelling manifestation until He went to His Father. That's what He said in John 16:7:

"NEVERTHELESS I TELL YOU THE TRUTH! IT IS EXPEDIENT FOR YOU THAT I GO AWAY, FOR IF I GO NOT AWAY THE COMFORTER WILL NOT COME UNTO YOU; BUT IF I DEPART, I WILL SEND HIM UNTO YOU."

Why was it expedient for Him to go away? Why was it to our advantage for Christ to go to His Father and to our Father? If you were there having the Last Supper with Him and He said,

"Listen to me now, it is to your distinct advantage that I go away, because if I do not go away the Comforter will not come, but if I go I will send Him unto you."

Would you believe that it was to your advantage that the Miracle Worker depart from the scene?

Why, who would heal the sick; who would raise the dead? Who would make new eyes for the blind, and who would feed the multitudes? There was only one Jesus, and no one ever spoke like He spoke, because He spoke as one having authority, and when He spoke, wonderful things happened. People were healed, the deaf heard, the lame walked, the blind saw, and the poor had the Gospel preached to them. How would those things happen if He went away?

Who was this Comforter that He kept talking about - the one Jesus was going to send? Is He the same One Jesus talked about in John 14:16-17, the One who was going to dwell in us? What did all this mean? Why was it to our advantage that Jesus go to His Father and that He send the Comforter?

And what did He mean in John 14:18?

"I WILL NOT LEAVE YOU AS ORPHANS, I WILL COME TO YOU."

THE BODY OF CHRIST NOW HAS MANY MEMBERS

Christ has a Body in Delaware, and a Body in Columbus. He has a Body in Tulsa, and a Body in San Francisco. He has a Body in Hong Kong, and a Body in Jerusalem. Since He is living in each one of these individual bodies, including yours, He now has all these brand new creatures to work through. John 14:17 and 23 say that the Father, the Son and the Holy Spirit are dwelling in every spirit-filled Believer. **"I will not leave you as orphans."** He has come to live in us. The fullness of the God Head dwells in you.

1 John 4:4 says,

"...GREATER IS HE WHO IS IN YOU, THAN HE WHO IS IN THE WORLD."

God is dwelling in you.

Since God is dwelling in you, and in every Believer, Jesus now has all these Bodies to work through -

to share His Love with others about salvation;
to share His Love about healing;
to share His Love about the baptism of the Holy
Spirit;
to share His Love about setting the captives
free; and to share His Love about the
acceptable year of the Lord with all who will
hear.

Jesus told us in Matthew 18:20,

**"FOR WHERE TWO OR THREE HAVE
GATHERED TOGETHER IN MY NAME, THERE
I AM IN THE MIDST OF YOU."**

He dwells in the midst of Believers, and do you remember that everywhere Jesus was He met people's needs! He always came to Minister! He never came to gossip, or to shoot the breeze, or just to kill some time.

He came to set the Captives free, to preach the Gospel, to heal the sick, to feed the multitudes, to minister to the needs of the people.

Since He and His Father have given the Holy Ghost to the Church, to His Body; He is not restricted to one specific Body of flesh and blood now - He has millions of Bodies all over the world to work through. And His Body will still do the same things it always did, and greater things through the One who dwells in the midst of all the Believers in every nation and on every Continent - even in the uttermost parts of the earth.

Can't you get excited about that?

That the Lord of Glory has chosen to dwell in you! That He has chosen to give you His precious Holy Spirit! And that He plans to use you in this final age to proclaim His Excellencies!

Praise God! It is a brand new ball game! You are in a fixed fight because Jesus fixed it for you in the end! You are in right standing with God. Don't you rejoice that the Bible tells you in 2 Corinthians 5:21:

"...That you are the righteousness of God in Christ Jesus."

You are in right standing with God. You are in good with God, and it is about time that you sent that old Inadequate - Unworthy - "I Can't Do It Spirit" - on its way so you can get on about living your life more abundantly in the Lord Jesus Christ. When you realize who you are, and what you are - when you realize who is living in you, you ought to have a superiority complex! You are a child of The King of Kings!

The Liar has lied to you long enough about being inferior, unworthy, and inadequate. The Bible says in 1 Corinthians 1:30:

"BUT BY HIS DOING YOU ARE IN CHRIST JESUS, WHO BECAME TO US WISDOM FROM GOD, AND RIGHTEOUSNESS AND SANCTIFICATION AND REDEMPTION."

Do you understand what the Holy Spirit is telling you? He said that Jesus Christ has been made unto you Wisdom - Jesus is your Wisdom, and that means that you have the wisdom of God. Do you know that ought to make you the smartest creature in three counties, or at least until you run into another born again, spirit-filled Believer, who is letting the Word of God become flesh in him.

Jesus is your **Redemption**, your **Sanctification**, your **Righteousness**, your **Wisdom**, and you are in good with God!

Hallelujah! If you are able to shout at ball games; or if you get excited about a new dress, or a song, or about a serving of fried okra, or about a piece of pecan pie ala mode - then surely you can get excited about your special relationship with God!

Do not let the garbage dealer dump any more garbage in your life. Turn in your franchise - tell him he is going to have to get a new local agent, tell him that you are not going to be his Garbage Dump anymore, because you are a brand new creature in Christ Jesus. You are a new Species, and you are taking every thought captive to the obedience of Christ!

You have been redeemed from the curse of the Law! You have been set free from every spirit of inadequacy. None of them can dwell in you, because you have been bought with a price, and now you are the Temple of the Holy Spirit. Do you know that God's Temple is full of His Anointing! There is not a single "Inadequate, Unworthy, I Can't Make It Spot" anyplace in the Temple of God. God's Temple - that is what you are - His special dwelling place. That is your new image.

I know you like that image a lot better than the old inadequacy image the devil has been dressing you with for so long.

SECTION III

CHAPTER TWELVE

HOW YOU CAN CONFUSE FAMILIAR SPIRITS.

Now that you know what Familiar Spirits are, and how they act; what do you do when they manifest themselves in your life? How do you handle them when they show up at your house, and begin to shake you up - to rattle your senses - and to roll you around in life?

Let me show you a method that always works - every time - it never fails - and it works on every kind of Spirit, Familiar or otherwise, because it is the Word of God. God's Word is the only thing that is infallible! I want to show you how you can confuse Familiar Spirits! I want to show you how you can make Familiar Spirits unfamiliar with you!

Let us look at Genesis 1:26 together:

"THEN GOD, SAID, 'LET US MAKE MAN IN OUR IMAGE, ACCORDING TO OUR LIKENESS; AND LET THEM RULE OVER ALL THE EARTH, AND OVER EVERY CREEPING THING THAT CREEPS ON THE EARTH.' "

Then in the next verse, God did what He said He was going to do.

*"He created us in His own image, and He
blessed us and gave us dominion over all the
works of His Hands."*

Do you believe that this is a prophetic Scripture?
Is the Lord prophesying in Genesis 1:26? Well - think
about it a little.

Has anyone ever taken dominion over all the works
of God's Hands? Over everything He made?

We know that everything belongs to God, because
the Bible says in Psalm 89:11-12,

**"THE HEAVENS ARE THINE, THE EARTH
ALSO IS THINE; THE WORLD AND ALL IT
CONTAINS. THOU HAST FOUNDED THEM.
THE NORTH AND THE SOUTH, THOU HAST
CREATED THEM: ..."**

For whom did God create the earth and all that it
contains? For the devil and his crowd? For the dope
pusher, the adulterer? - For the ones who do not know
or even acknowledge God? Of course not! The devil
was not even in the world God created, because when
God finished His creation and looked at it, He said it
was good. The devil got in the world God created for
us by deception and by sin. He deceived Eve, and then
when Adam intentionally sinned, he (Adam) opened the
door to satan and surrendered the rights God had given
him to rule the earth.

Satan invaded! He had a plan of attack, he
followed his plan, and his plan worked.

Romans 5:12 sets forth this fact clearly:

"THEREFORE, JUST AS THROUGH ONE MAN SIN ENTERED INTO THE WORLD, AND DEATH THROUGH SIN, AND SO DEATH SPREAD TO ALL MEN, BECAUSE ALL SINNED ..."

Sin entered the world through one man! Sin entered through Adam's intentional sin. There was no sin, sickness, or death in this world until Adam sinned and allowed satan to come into God's Kingdom. But none of the basic facts of creation have changed; as created, God made the world for us! He made the world and the fullness thereof for Believers - for the ones He talked about in 2 Corinthians 6:16-18, in Leviticus 26:12, Exodus 29:45, Jeremiah 31:31-34, and other Scriptures. My brief paraphrase of the thoughts contained in these verses would be,

"God said, One day I am going to have me a people!" "I am going to walk in them, and I am going to live in them." "I am going to be their God, and they are going to be my people!"

The Bible says that God has a people, and in addition to having a people, He has a plan for them. Thank God that His plan for His people is good! God does not have a bad plan for you. He made the world for us and all the fullness thereof, but for the last 2,000 years the Church (God's People) has been concentrating on receiving the message of Poor, Broke, Inadequate, Sick, and Hungry that the devil has been broadcasting to them on every wave length. We have been good receivers all right, unfortunately we have been "tuned-in" to the wrong source. We need to change channels.

Many people in the Church have been deceived by the devil- just like Eve was - and those who have been deceived have never really believed what God said about His creation in Genesis 1:26:

"LET US MAKE MAN IN OUR IMAGE...AND GIVE THEM DOMINION OVER ALL THE WORKS OF OUR HANDS."

The Holy Spirit told Paul to talk to us about unbelief in Romans 3:3-4. Paul used the children of Israel as an illustration. In these Scriptures he reminds us of the opportunities they had to believe what God told them - some did and some did not, and Paul said,

"WHAT THEN? IF SOME DID NOT BELIEVE, THEIR UNBELIEF WILL NOT NULLIFY THE FAITHFULNESS OF GOD, WILL IT? MAY IT NEVER BE! RATHER, LET GOD BE FOUND TRUE, THOUGH EVERY MAN BE FOUND A LIAR, AS IT IS WRITTEN, ..."

Paul said .... "So what if some did not believe!" Their unbelief or your unbelief will not change the truthfulness of God's Word.

God's Word is always true whether you believe it or not. Let me give you an example, the truth about salvation was the truth about salvation long before you believed the truth and were saved! And that truth is still the truth today! Since the truth about salvation was the truth before you knew this truth - Do you suppose there just might be some other truths in His Word that you have not received because you do not know the truth about them?

The Holy Spirit is also instructing us to take our eyes off of people and to keep them firmly fixed on the Lord. Listen carefully to me now -

"Paul said, do not let someone else's unbelief mess you up!"

Because they did not believe God's Word does not mean that you can not believe His Word. It is your choice, you can believe or you can believe not! Because they failed to receive what was promised in God's Word does not mean that you must fail.

God is true! And His Word is the truth! The truth records the fact that you were made in the image and likeness of God, and that God has given you dominion over all the works of His hands. You can accept that truth or reject it!

WHAT YOU ARE IN CHRIST DEPENDS ON YOU!

Does God really mean what He says? Well, of course He does. He says what He means and means what He says, and one of the things He said in Mark 16:15-16 is:

"GO YE INTO ALL THE WORLD AND PREACH THE GOSPEL TO EVERY CREATURE. HE THAT BELIEVETH AND IS BAPTIZED SHALL BE SAVED, BUT HE THAT BELIEVETH NOT SHALL BE DAMNED."

This Scripture is very straightforward. It contains both affirmative and negative promises. You can be saved or you can be damned! Do you realize that what you are depends on you - on what you do with God's Word? It is easy to see that in this Scripture, isn't it?

You can believe and be saved, or you can believe not and be damned!

You have a choice on what you do with God's Word. You can leave it on the shelf, or you can put His Word in you. You have your "druthers"! Have you ever had your druthers? Why, you have them every day by choosing,

what you do with your life;
what you do with your time;
what you do with your money;
and by choosing what you do with your thought
life and your tongue!

You make a choice everyday about what you are going to do and about how you are going to live. It does not make any difference whether you acknowledge it with your mouth or not, your whole life-style acknowledges your choice! You have a choice on what you are in Christ! You have your druthers on what you do with the Word of God.

What you are in Christ then, depends on you!

What you do with God's Word does not depend on your pastor, or on your spouse, or on your mother-in-law. What you do with God's Word does not even depend on God. Why doesn't it depend on God? What you are in Christ does not depend on God because God has done what He promised to do - He sent His Son as the final sacrifice for sin. Remember when Jesus was on the Cross? In John 19:30 He shouted,

"IT IS FINISHED!"

and the Veil of the Temple was rent in twain, from the top to the bottom! You now have access to the Father through the Blood of the Lamb who was slain from the foundation of the World. "IT IS FINISHED!", Jesus shouted triumphantly. He did all that His Father sent Him to do. Now it is up to you. Your spouse, or your pastor, or your friends may help you, or they may be a hindrance to you - But what you are in Christ is up to you!

The Bible says in 2 Corinthians 5:19:

"....GOD WAS IN CHRIST RECONCILING THE WORLD TO HIMSELF, NOT COUNTING THEIR TRESPASSES AGAINST THEM...."

God, through Christ, has reconciled you to Himself. He has restored you to favor. The relationship that was broken through sin (Romans 5:12), has now been restored through the Blood shed by the Lamb of God at Calvary! Those in Christ - All of His New Creatures - Have been reconciled to God. You are Reconciled! Justified! - Just as if you had never sinned. All of the rights and privileges that were lost by Adam when he intentionally sinned, have been restored through Christ Jesus our Lord. In fact, the Bible says you and I now have a better Covenant than anyone ever had before Christ!

But the devil does not want you to know what your rights are in Christ! He will try to deceive you, so he can keep you in the dark about who you are, and the authority you have over him now, in this life. He will try to lord it over you. 2 Corinthians 4:4 calls the devil,

"THE GOD OF THIS WORLD...," and some Christians use this Scripture along with some others to say,

> "I just cannot make it here on earth because the Bible says that satan is the god of this world, and since he is the god of this world he has control over me. And I am not strong enough to resist him."

Well, that is partially true, satan is the god of this world! But the good part is - You are strong enough to resist him in Christ! And you must realize that the god of this world is the "god of the world", but that does not mean that he is your God. The devil is not your god, is he? Say that with me, will you?

"The god of this world is not my God!"

Do you know why the god of this world is not your God? It is because the Father, the Son and the Holy Spirit is your God. You belong to the God of all Creation. The Bible says in Colossians 1:13:

"FOR HE DELIVERED US FROM THE DOMAIN OF DARKNESS, AND TRANSFERRED US TO THE KINGDOM OF HIS BELOVED SON."

The god of this world is not your God because you have been delivered out of his power. You were delivered from his domain and his authority when you received Christ as your Savior. That was a promotion! - You were promoted when you were born again! Have you accepted this promotion in your life? - Have you accepted your deliverance from the devil's power and authority over you?

Let's think about Genesis 1:26 for a moment.

"LET US MAKE MAN IN OUR OWN IMAGE AND GIVE HIM DOMINION OVER ALL THE WORKS OF OUR HANDS."

Has anyone ever taken dominion over all the works of God's Hands? Did Adam take dominion? Is he the one God made the world for? Well, God did make the world for Adam and for us, but we know that Adam did not take total dominion, because he sinned; so he did not fulfill this Scripture in his life. If not Adam, who then?

When we study the Scriptures we can see some instances of partial dominion in the Bible:

MOSES - when the Red Sea parted;

JOSHUA - when the sun stood still;

ELIJAH - when the widow woman's meal barrel and her bottle of oil refused to be empty;

ELISHA - when the Shumanite woman's son was restored to life;

DAVID - when he defeated Goliath in the name of JEHOVAH-SABAOTH! - The Lord of Hosts;

PETER AND JOHN - when they commanded the crippled man to walk in the name of Jesus Christ at the gate called Beautiful.

All of these men took partial dominion, but the only One who ever took total dominion over all the works of God's Hands is the Lord Jesus Christ!

*He took dominion over the elements when He
rebuked the Spirits that caused the storm on
the Sea of Galilee.
He commanded, "PEACE BE STILL!"
He took dominion over material matter when
He broke the bread and fed the multitudes!
He took dominion over sickness and disease
when He healed the sick, and when He set the
captives free!
He took dominion over death when He shouted,
"LAZARUS - COME FORTH!"
Jesus took dominion over all the Works of
God's Hands!*

Aren't you glad someone did? And aren't you glad
that that someone was the Son of God, the One who
came so we could have life, and life more abundantly?
It would be tragic if God made the world and filled it
with all this good stuff, and then not a single one of His
Children ever enjoyed or experienced what God
created for us. - If none of His Creations enjoyed His
Creation in all its fullness!

Have we, as the Church, been a disappointment to
God? Have we ever fully understood and accepted our
rights in Christ? Are we willing to take dominion over
all the works of His Hands?

CHAPTER THIRTEEN

THE BIBLE MAKES SOME REMARKABLE STATEMENTS.

The Bible makes some remarkable statements. Let me share one of them with you that is recorded in Romans 8:29:

"FOR WHOM HE FOREKNEW, HE ALSO PREDESTINED TO BECOME CONFORMED TO THE IMAGE OF HIS SON, THAT HE MIGHT BE THE FIRST BORN AMONG MANY BRETHREN."

That really is a remarkable Scripture, isn't it? God plans for someone - Is it you? - to be conformed to the image of His Son.

Lots of us seem to remember Romans 8:28, but we almost never go on to 8:29. Remember 8:28? It says:

"AND WE KNOW THAT GOD CAUSES ALL THINGS TO WORK TOGETHER FOR GOOD TO THOSE WHO LOVE GOD, TO THOSE WHO ARE CALLED ACCORDING TO HIS PURPOSE."

This is a Scripture we can hang on to when something bad happens; when something happens that we do not understand. I thank God for it. This

Word from The Lord has been my fortress many times when the only things I could see with my senses were the storm clouds surrounding me!

Now the Bible does not say that everything that happens is good! Many things that happen in life are bad. This Scripture says, **"GOD CAUSES ALL THINGS TO WORK TOGETHER FOR GOOD TO THOSE WHO LOVE GOD..."**

Perhaps one of the most misunderstood words in the Bible is love. The Biblical definition of "loving God", is keeping His Word. That is true - Biblical love as it is used in Romans 8:28 does not have anything to do with your emotions, it is referring to your obedience to God's Word.

Let me give you some Scripture references. In John 14:21 Jesus said, **"IF YOU LOVE ME, YOU WILL KEEP MY COMMANDMENTS."** That is very easy to understand, isn't it. Do you love God? If you do, Jesus said you would keep His Commandments. In John 14:23 Jesus said, **"IF A MAN LOVE ME, HE WILL KEEP MY WORDS..."** In I John 5:3 the Holy Spirit recorded, **"FOR THIS IS THE LOVE OF GOD, THAT WE KEEP HIS COMMANDMENTS ..."** Some other references are John 14:15 and 2 John 6.

When you study these Scriptures, you will see that your love for God is determined by one thing, and by one thing only - are you keeping His Word? And if you are keeping His Word, if you are obedient, and if you do not give up and quit - God will make all things work together for good for you as you continue to love Him by keeping His Commandments! God said He would make the bad, good! Isn't that a magnificent promise?

To paraphrase - The Bible says God will cause all things to work together for good to those who keep His Word.

Let me give you an example. It was not good when Paul and Silas were whipped and thrown in jail in Philippi for casting out a demon spirit of divination! Do you remember what happened? This account is recorded in Acts 16. Here, these two servants of the Lord were having a miracle service in the middle of the street, and they got the devil so upset when they cast his spirit out of the slave girl, that the devil had them whipped and thrown in jail.

Surely you do not think it was God who caused this girl's masters to go into a rage because she could not tell fortunes anymore, do you? Of course it was not.

It was the devil!

And when he had them arrested, the devil probably thought that that was the end of that! I am glad it was not you or me in this situation, instead of Paul and Silas, aren't you? What would your reaction have been? Would you have cried out to God and said,

"LORD, why did you let this terrible thing happen to me? Remember me, I am your servant, the one the Holy Spirit spoke to and sent on this missionary journey. Here I was, doing my job, preaching the Gospel, casting out evil spirits, and just when I was about to get a good meeting going - just when things were about to break loose, I got arrested, and whipped, and then they threw me in jail!

Why me Lord? You know I am one of your good guys!"

Would you have been mad at God? Would you have pouted a little? Climbed up your miff tree, maybe?

Thank God, Paul and Silas did not react that way. They were not pouting, or murmuring, or complaining. Do you remember what they did when these "bad" things happened to them? - They started Praising God! And in the midst of their praising, God sent an earthquake and set them free.

DID IT WORK FOR GOOD FOR PAUL AND SILAS?

Did these bad things work for good for Paul and Silas? Sure they did! God caused these things to work together for good for Paul and Silas because they were faithful - they did not quit when the going got tough. They did not give up when something happened that they did not understand. And because of their faithfulness, they not only participated in a miracle of salvation when the Philippian Jailer and his whole household were saved; the Holy Ghost used this earth-shaking occasion to record a tremendous promise for the Church in Acts 16:31,

"...BELIEVE IN THE LORD JESUS, AND YOU SHALL BE SAVED, YOU AND YOUR HOUSEHOLD."

The Holy Ghost told us how to get our households saved - We can believe for them! That does not mean that we can receive Christ for them, but it does mean we can believe for their Salvation. We can believe for their deliverance, we can commit them to the Lord.

We can deal with the spirits who are keeping our loved ones out of the Kingdom of God! Thank God we have some rights in Christ if we will accept them. Our rights in Christ are manifested when we have enough determination to learn God's Word, to act on God's Word, and then to stand firm on His Word.

Every man, every woman, every person has to receive Christ for themselves. I can not receive Christ as Savior for you or for my children, but Praise God, I can reach a place in Christ where I can believe for them. I can fight the Spiritual forces that are keeping them out of the Kingdom of God. You will have to fight for them, because your unsaved loved ones not only do not know how to fight, they do not have any weapons with which to fight! They are not armed to do battle with the devil!

Paul said in 2 Corinthians 10:4,

"FOR THE WEAPONS OF OUR WARFARE ARE NOT OF THE FLESH, BUT DIVINELY POWERFUL FOR THE DESTRUCTION OF FORTRESSES..."

KJ "FOR THE WEAPONS OF OUR WARFARE ARE NOT CARNAL, ..."

People who are not saved do not have any weapons to use to fight with the devil! They are carnal - of the flesh - they do not know anything about spiritual weapons. They are unarmed, and that makes them defenseless. They do not know how to fight, but thank God, the Holy Ghost has a game plan on how you can get your household saved.

You can believe for them! You can stand against the spirits who are keeping them out of the Kingdom of God.

God wants to save them. That is why the Lord Jesus Christ was crucified - to save sinners! So you need to stop running around telling everyone who will listen to you, "My husband - or my wife - or my children - or my parents - are not saved."

You need to get in the trenches and begin to fight a few battles for your loved ones. Remember this Scripture in Acts 16:31 said, "...Your household"! It did not say everyone on the block, or in the next three counties, or far away in Africa, or someone you knew 39 years ago. The Holy Spirit is talking about your household! God has given every Believer the authority to believe for his family. The Bible says in Isaiah 49:25 that when you get your life in right standing with God, He will save your children! If you have children, you will love this promise! If you will apply His Word to you - you will win.

The Bible says in Acts 16:25-26,

"BUT ABOUT MIDNIGHT PAUL AND SILAS WERE PRAYING AND SINGING HYMNS OF PRAISE TO GOD, AND THE PRISONERS WERE LISTENING TO THEM; AND SUDDENLY THERE CAME A GREAT EARTHQUAKE, SO THAT ALL THE FOUNDATIONS OF THE PRISON HOUSE WERE SHAKEN; AND IMMEDIATELY ALL THE DOORS WERE OPENED, AND EVERYONE'S CHAINS WERE UNFASTENED."

Paul and Silas were praising God at midnight, and you know they were praising Him right out loud with their mouths because everyone was listening. You cannot hear silent praise with your ears. And all the other prisoners heard them and so did the jailer because he wanted to know what he must do to be saved.

I wonder what time they started praising God....11:59 p.m.? 11:50 p.m., maybe? 9:30, 8:00, 6:15 p.m.? How long were Paul and Silas going to continue to Praise The Lord? Do you think they were going to praise God until the prison doors opened for them?

How is it in your life? Do you ever praise God? Are you determined to continue to praise Him until the prison doors open in your life? Until you have the answer in your spirit? Do you have a limit on praise? Is praise on a budget in your life?

Paul and Silas were not praising God for the bad! They were not praising Him because they had been whipped and thrown in jail. God is not the one who had them jailed! They were praising God because He had saved them! They were praising God because He had delivered them from the Power of Darkness! They were praising God because He had filled them with His Holy Spirit! They were praising God because they knew He had a much better plan for them, than the

"Old whipped and bleeding and locked in the stocks"

situation that they found themselves in at the moment. They were praising God because He was God! They were not praising Him for the bad - they were praising Him for the good He had in mind for them.

They were praising Him for the promises He had made to them that had not yet been manifested in their lives! That is one of the secrets of praise! You can praise God for the promises He has made to you in His Word that have not yet been manifested in your life.

What promises? Well, every promise! The Bible says in 2 Corinthians 1:20,

"FOR ALL THE PROMISES OF GOD IN HIM ARE YEA, AND IN HIM AMEN, UNTO THE GLORY OF GOD BY US."

Every promise of God is in Christ, Yes, and Amen! The Bible says every single one of them in Christ are "...YEA AND...AMEN!" Surely you can praise Him for that.

Get into God's Word. That is where His Promises are recorded. Find out what God promised you, and then begin to thank Him for His promises. Thank Him for fulfilling His promises in your life!

What would have happened if Paul and Silas had quit before they had been set free?

What would have happened if they had given up? Would everything have worked together for good? Of course not! God causes all things to work together for good when we continue in His Word! We are to be doers of the Word and not hearers only, whether we understand the situation we are in at the moment or not. God will cause all things to work together for good when we are faithful to His Word.

That is what this book is all about, Spiritual Warfare!

Thank God, it works; all of my children are saved and filled with His Holy Spirit. You have the right to believe for your household.

Let's look at 2 Corinthians 1:20 again,

"FOR ALL THE PROMISES OF GOD IN HIM ARE YEA, AND IN HIM AMEN."

Did you notice where the promises are? They are in Christ! Did you also notice that the answer is not yes, or no, or maybe? Have you ever heard that God answers prayers with a no or a maybe sometimes? Do not let junky teaching like this keep you out of your Promised Land. Listen, this Scripture says that every single one of God's Promises to the Believer are Yea and Amen in Christ! If God's Promises are not being manifested in your life, then you must examine yourself to see where you are dwelling. Is it in Christ?

Do you remember John 15:7?

"IF YOU ABIDE IN ME AND MY WORDS ABIDE IN YOU, ASK WHATEVER YOU WISH, AND IT SHALL BE DONE FOR YOU."

God's promises include salvation for your loved ones, health for your body, peace in your family, and food for your table, among other things. Don't let the devil trick you into taking second, or third, or thirty-ninth best. God said the answer to each and every one of His promises in Christ is Yea and Amen. That means YES and YES indeed!

When do you get all these promises? Are they free? Do you have to do anything? Do they come automatically when you receive Christ as your Savior?

Now let's go on from Romans 8:28 to Romans 8:29.

"FOR WHOM HE FOREKNEW, HE ALSO PREDESTINED TO BECOME CONFORMED

TO THE IMAGE OF HIS SON, THAT HE MIGHT BE THE FIRST BORN AMONG MANY BRETHREN."

"Aw, surely God doesn't mean me." "That Scripture does not really mean that God expects me to become conformed - for me to be like His Son, the Lord Jesus Christ, does it?"

You are not thinking thoughts like that, are you?

Now before you begin to get spooky on me with words like foreknew and predestined, let me tell you what the Holy Spirit means by them.

Some folks think predestined means that their fate and their future is already determined, and it does not make any difference what they do ...

"Oh, I am just destined to float along in the clouds, brother."

"My destiny is to be a loser, it does not make any difference how hard I try, my fate has already been determined."

"I have to read my daily horoscope to find out what I am supposed to do today."

They ought to change that title to "Horror-Scope" because God tells us over and over again in His Word not to mess around with that stuff because it is of the devil. Read Deuteronomy 18:9-14. God said, "Trust in Me, not in the planets or the stars, or fortune tellers, or necromancers, or any of their traveling companions."

What do those words mean, then? Foreknew and Predestined?.

The Scriptures will interpret themselves if we will look at them, and spend a little time studying the Word. The more of God's Word that you have in you, the more of God's Word you will understand. Amen? Amen.

Let us look at the Scripture in Ephesians 1:4-5,

"JUST AS HE CHOSE US IN HIM BEFORE THE FOUNDATION OF THE WORLD, THAT WE SHOULD BE HOLY AND BLAMELESS BEFORE HIM IN LOVE.

HE PREDESTINED US TO ADOPTION AS SONS THROUGH JESUS CHRIST TO HIMSELF, ACCORDING TO THE KIND INTENTION OF HIS WILL."

The Bible says God chose us in Him before the foundation of the world - and He predestined us to adoption as sons.

What is the Biblical meaning of foreknew? Foreknow means to know beforehand. The Lord knew, before the foundation of the world, that you would respond to His message of Love. He knew you would receive Christ as your personal Savior. God is not dumb. He is not in doubt about the future - His Future, your future, or the devil's future. He knew that you would choose to come to Him before He made the world. He chose you in Him before the foundation of the world ... He knew you beforehand, He foreknew you before you became flesh.

Do not try to relate this to some theology about divine election - that God has elected some to salvation, and that He has elected some to damnation.

The election is ours! We have the right to have our druthers. Remember Mark 16:15, we can believe or we can believe not! It is our choice, and we make choices and elections everyday by what we do. We elect to read the Word, or we elect to watch TV. We elect to get up, or we elect to be "holy-rollers" and just roll over in bed and go back to sleep instead of getting up to go to Church. We elect to fast or we elect to eat. We elect to gossip or we elect to control our tongues as James instructed us to do.

God does not make these elections for us, we make them ourselves.

The Lord has given us this unusual phenomenon called a "Freewill." We have the right to do what we want to do. Do you realize that God never takes our freewill away from us? We always have the right to do what we want to do, before we are saved, and after we are saved. It is our choice, and we will continue to make our own elections until we see Him face to face.

Does this foreknew Scripture mean then, that it is God's plan to save only a select few?

Well, let's see what the Scriptures say about God's plan to save all or just a select few. In 2 Peter 3:9, The Holy Spirit said,

"...NOT WISHING FOR ANY TO PERISH BUT FOR ALL TO COME TO REPENTANCE."

All does mean ALL, doesn't it? If it does, then the Bible says it is not God's Pre-Determined Will that any should perish. It is not your destiny - God has not destined that you perish because the Scripture says in John 3:16,

"FOR GOD SO LOVED THE WORLD THAT HE GAVE HIS ONLY BEGOTTEN SON, THAT WHOSOEVER BELIEVETH IN HIM SHOULD NOT PERISH, BUT HAVE EVERLASTING LIFE."

Christ's sacrifice is sufficient for all. For all who were, for all who presently are, and for all who ever will be!

And God expresses His Will again in 1 Timothy 2:4,

"WHO DESIRES ALL MEN TO BE SAVED AND TO COME TO THE KNOWLEDGE OF THE TRUTH."

There's the word ALL again. God desires all men to be saved! Not some, but all. We sing a song sometimes that contains the words, "There's room at the cross for you." Thank God it is true - there is room at the Cross for everyone - regardless of your sex, or race, or color; there is room at the Cross for you!

How about predestined then, what does this word mean?

Predestined means "Pre-Determined." God's Pre-determined Will was that you receive the Lord Jesus Christ as your personal Savior. That is His plan for you and it is His plan for every person! God always knew what His plan was for you, and He always knew what His plan was for all flesh.

And then after you are born again, it is His pre-determined will that you become conformed to the image of His Son. That is what He is talking about in Romans 8:29,

"He also predestined (His predetermined plan is for) every Believer to become conformed to the image of His Son."

God's plan for you and for everyone is that every new creature will be conformed to the image of His Son.

Isn't that tremendous!

The Creator, the Lord of Lords, the King of Kings, the One who spoke the worlds into existence, also spoke you into existence. And our Almighty God's Pre-determined plan when He spoke you into existence was for "poor little old insignificant you" to be conformed to the image of His Son, the Lord Jesus Christ.

Aren't you thrilled that the One who knows all things, that the One in whom all wisdom and knowledge resides, that the One whose name is Wonderful Counselor - said that He had enough confidence in His Ability in you, that you could be conformed to the image of His Son! Imagine that!

Hebrews 11:3 says,

"...THE WORLDS WERE MADE BY THE WORD OF GOD..."!

The same Word of God that made the world said that it is His pre-determined plan that you be like His Son. When you comprehend this fact - your life will change.

You do remember His Son don't you? Sure you do. He is the only one who ever took dominion over all the works of His Father's Hands. God anticipates that you will be like Jesus. He did not make you to suffer and die on Calvary; there is only one Messiah! But God did make you to take dominion over all the works of His Hands!

He is convinced that His creative Word will work in you, just like it worked in creating the worlds from the things not seen.

That really is Good News, isn't it!

CHAPTER FOURTEEN

HOW DID JESUS GET TO BE JESUS ?

How did Jesus get to be Jesus? Was He born a baby, or was He born full grown?

We do know the answer to that question. Jesus was born a baby, because the Bible says in Luke 2:7,

"AND SHE GAVE BIRTH TO HER FIRST-BORN SON: AND SHE WRAPPED HIM IN CLOTHS, AND LAID HIM IN A MANGER, BECAUSE THERE WAS NO ROOM FOR THEM IN THE INN."

She laid Him in a manger. Mary treated Him like a baby because He was a baby. Luke 2:16 records,

"THE SHEPHERDS CAME IN HASTE AND FOUND THEIR WAY TO MARY AND JOSEPH AND THE BABY AS HE LAY IN THE MANGER."

Jesus, The Son Of God, was a baby when He was born; He was born the Messiah - but He had to grow up! He could not remain a baby all of His life, and still do the things the Prophets prophesied about Him. A baby could not do all those things. Jesus had to grow up! He had to mature! A baby could not:

Be wounded for our transgressions, or be bruised for our iniquities; a baby could not take the chastisement of our peace upon Him, and take stripes for our healing.

These are some of the things Isaiah said the Messiah would do in Isaiah 53:5. Jesus had to grow up, He could not remain a baby all of His life and accomplish the things that He and His Father planned for Him to do. You remember what He came to do, don't you?

Jesus said in John 10:10,

"...I CAME THAT THEY MIGHT HAVE LIFE, AND MIGHT HAVE IT MORE ABUNDANTLY."

Jesus came to give us abundant life. Babies cannot do that, can they? Babies do bring joy and love and happiness into our lives, but babies cannot defeat the devil because they do not know how to fight!

All babies have one thing in common - they want their own way! In fact they will insist on having their own way. They will cry for their bottles, or cry for some attention. They never get up to clean the house, or to wash the dishes; they never crawl out of their cribs and go to work to buy some food, or to pay the bills. They are babies; and the only desire they know and experience for some period of time is having their needs met. Babies are babies and they are always concerned about their own wants and needs.

In Acts 10:38, Peter summarizing Jesus' ministry to Cornelius, said,

"YOU KNOW OF JESUS OF NAZARETH, HOW GOD ANOINTED HIM WITH THE HOLY SPIRIT AND WITH POWER, AND HOW HE WENT ABOUT DOING GOOD, AND HEALING ALL WHO WERE OPPRESSED BY THE DEVIL; FOR GOD WAS WITH HIM."

God anointed Jesus with the Holy Ghost and with power, and He went about doing good for others, not for Himself. Jesus went about helping others! Think about that for a minute or two. Jesus thought of others first.

Then John said in 1 John 3:8,

"...FOR THIS PURPOSE THE SON OF GOD WAS MANIFESTED, THAT HE MIGHT DESTROY THE WORKS OF THE DEVIL."

Babies do not do things like this, do they? Babies think about themselves first - they do not think about the needs of others. Jesus grew up so He could be all that He and His Father planned for Him to be. He grew up so He could defeat the devil and to fulfill all the prophecies about The Messiah!

Now continue to think with me for a minute, will you? Since it is God's Pre-determined Will (since it is your destiny) that you be conformed to the image of His Son, then you will have to grow up, won't you?

Since His Son grew up, then you will have to grow up to be like Him.

Well - how did Jesus do it? How did He grow up? We know He grew, because the Bible says in Luke 2:40,

"AND THE CHILD CONTINUED TO GROW AND BECOME STRONG, INCREASING IN WISDOM; AND THE GRACE OF GOD WAS UPON HIM."

Jesus continued to grow! Do you remember when He was twelve? We talked about this before, but let us look at this in a little more depth. His parents went to Jerusalem to celebrate the Passover, and they unintentionally left Jerusalem without Him. They traveled a whole day before they discovered that He was not with them. You have never done that, have you? Gone your own way without the Lord? Have you ever traveled for a day or a week maybe, or even for a whole month, or a year without the Lord? Some folks do their own thing all their lives - they never miss the Lord until it is too late.

Well, Joseph and Mary missed Him, and they went back to Jerusalem and searched for Him for three days before they found Him. In Luke 2:46-47, the Bible says He was,

"...IN THE TEMPLE SITTING IN THE MIDST OF THE TEACHERS, BOTH LISTENING TO THEM AND ASKING THEM QUESTIONS. AND ALL WHO HEARD HIM WERE AMAZED AT HIS UNDERSTANDING AND HIS ANSWERS."

He was only 12, but they were all amazed at His understanding and knowledge of God and the Scriptures.

When His parents found Him in the Temple, they told Him how concerned they had been about Him, and how they had looked all over Jerusalem for Him for

three whole days. His reply was startling! In Luke 2:49
He said,

**"...DID YOU NOT KNOW THAT I HAD TO BE
ABOUT MY FATHER'S BUSINESS?"**

God has a business! And Jesus was about it!
God's business with Jesus was for Him to grow up and
learn His Word. His business with you, now that you
are saved is exactly the same. God wants you to grow
up and learn His Word. The only way you can be
conformed to the image of His Son is through His
Word! That is God's business, and that should be your
business, too.

Jesus is the Word of God - that is what the Bible
says in John 1:1, so what else would God use to
conform you to His Son's Image except His Word. Luke
2:52 says,

**"AND JESUS KEPT INCREASING IN WISDOM
AND STATURE, AND IN FAVOR WITH GOD
AND MEN."**

He kept increasing, He did not stop. Even when all
who heard Him were amazed at His understanding, and
at His answers, He did not quit! He kept right on about
His Father's business! He continued to grow and
increase in wisdom!

He kept studying and learning and doing the Word
of God until one day He became Conformed to the
Image of His Father. You know He did, because in
John 14:9 He told Phillip,

"...HE WHO HAS SEEN ME HAS SEEN THE FATHER."

He looked and acted like His Father.

Well, specifically - how did He do it; how did Jesus get to be like God? He was born a flesh and blood baby just like we are, but somehow He became like His Father.

Did Jesus have an image that He conformed to? Did He have a goal in His life? Did Jesus really become conformed to the Image of God?

What do the Scriptures say Christ was like? Let's look at the Biblical description of Jesus. 2 Corinthians 4:4 tells us that Christ is the image of God.

"...THAT THEY MIGHT NOT SEE THE LIGHT OF THE GOSPEL OF THE GLORY OF CHRIST, WHO IS THE IMAGE OF GOD."

Colossians 1:15 states,

"AND HE IS THE IMAGE OF THE INVISIBLE GOD, THE FIRST BORN OF ALL CREATION."

"AND HE IS THE RADIANCE OF HIS GLORY AND THE EXACT REPRESENTATION OF HIS NATURE, AND UPHOLDS ALL THINGS BY THE WORD OF HIS POWER..." Hebrews 1:3

The King James translation reads, "...THE EXPRESS IMAGE OF HIS PERSON, ..." The Bible says that Jesus Christ, the Messiah, was the express image

of God. Jesus conformed to the Image of His Father.
John 1:1:

**"IN THE BEGINNING WAS THE WORD, AND
THE WORD WAS WITH GOD, AND THE WORD
WAS GOD."**

How did He do it?
How did Jesus conform to the Image of His Father?
He was born a baby, with baby hands and baby feet.
He had a baby mind and thought baby thoughts; but
somehow He became just like His Father. And if we
can see how He did it, we will understand how we can
become conformed to His Image. Romans 8:29 says
that is God's Will for us, and since all of us want to
please God, let's get on with our study.

HOW JESUS GOT TO BE JESUS!

Our source is the Bible, and the Bible was written
for our instruction, so let us look at some Scriptures
together to see what the Lord's thought pattern was -
so we can see how He reacted to situations - so we can
see how He became conformed to the Image of God.
John 5:19 says,

**"JESUS SAID, TRULY, TRULY, I SAY TO YOU,
THE SON CAN DO NOTHING OF HIMSELF,
UNLESS IT IS SOMETHING HE SEES THE
FATHER DOING; FOR WHATEVER THE
FATHER DOES, THESE THINGS THE SON
ALSO DOES IN LIKE MANNER."**

Would you have thought that about Jesus? That He could only do what He saw His Father doing? The Son of God - the Holy One of Israel - the One born of a Virgin - the Messiah said,

> "*I can do nothing of myself unless it is something I see my Father doing.*"

Then in John 5:30 Jesus said,

> **"I CAN DO NOTHING ON MY OWN INITIATIVE. AS I HEAR, I JUDGE; AND MY JUDGMENT IS JUST, BECAUSE I DO NOT SEEK MY OWN WILL, BUT THE WILL OF HIM WHO SENT ME."**

The King James translation reads, **"I CAN OF MY OWN SELF DO NOTHING."**

Does this Scripture sound a little more like you sometimes? "I cannot do it!" Well, Jesus said He could not do it either when He relied on His own ability. But Jesus did not attempt to rely on His own ability; He relied on God's ability! He did not seek His own will; He only did the will of His Father.

Want to look at some more Scriptures with me?

> **"...I DO NOTHING ON MY OWN INITIATIVE."**
> **John 8:28**

Jesus did nothing on His own initiative. That means He followed His Father's instructions. He was obedient. And finally after the Jews continued to contend with Him, He said in John 10:37 and 38,

"IF I DO NOT DO THE WORKS OF MY FATHER, DO NOT BELIEVE ME; BUT IF I DO THEM, THOUGH YOU DO NOT BELIEVE ME, BELIEVE THE WORKS THAT YOU MAY KNOW AND UNDERSTAND THAT THE FATHER IS IN ME, AND I IN THE FATHER."

Do you realize what all this means?
It means that when the leper in Luke 5:12 said,

"...LORD, IF YOU ARE WILLING, YOU CAN MAKE ME CLEAN."

And Jesus stretched out His hand, and touched him saying,

"I AM WILLING,"

Jesus was declaring His Father's will about Healing. He said what His Father told Him to say, and He did what He saw His Father doing! That means Jesus saw His Father healing that leper! It was a miracle of God, and He said, "If you do not believe Me, at least believe the Works."

Since Jesus only did what His Father told Him to do, do you realize that He was expressing God's Will,

When He made new eyes for the man born blind in the 9th Chapter of John. His Father must have spoken to Him and said, "Son, make that man some new eyes!" Because Jesus said He only did what His Father told Him to do.

When He told the man whose friends had torn
the roof off to get to Him,
"RISE AND WALK."
He was saying exactly what His Father told Him
to say;
That when He healed the sick, when He raised
the dead, when He fed the multitudes - that He
was doing what He saw His Father doing, and
He was doing what His Father told Him to do.

"...I CAN DO NOTHING ON MY OWN
INITIATIVE,.."

He said. He repeated this same message in John
12:49, and again in John 14:10 and 11. Jesus
depended on His Father's ability to do the Works that
He did. He did not depend on Himself. He did not
depend on His own ability. Jesus depended and relied
on His Father's ability in Him to get the job done in
every situation.

He and His Father were One!

Do you know who He is depending on to do His
Works in you? Jesus prayed in John 17:17-21,

"SANCTIFY THEM IN THE TRUTH; THY WORD
IS TRUTH,
AS THOU DIDST SEND ME INTO THE WORLD,
I ALSO HAVE SENT THEM INTO THE WORLD.
AND FOR THEIR SAKES, I SANCTIFY
MYSELF, THAT THEY THEMSELVES ALSO
MAY BE SANCTIFIED IN TRUTH.
I DO NOT ASK IN BEHALF OF THESE ALONE,
BUT FOR THOSE ALSO WHO BELIEVE IN ME
THROUGH THEIR WORD;

**(He is praying for you and me now) THAT
THEY MAY ALL BE ONE; EVEN AS THOU,
FATHER, ARE IN ME AND I IN THEE, THAT
THEY ALSO MAY BE IN US;
THAT THE WORLD MAY BELIEVE THAT THOU
DIDST SEND ME."**

I know you are excited about that! Jesus is asking
the Father to let us do the Works of God. Remember,
He expressed the same thought in John 14:12,

**"VERILY, VERILY, I SAY UNTO YOU, HE THAT
BELIEVETH ON ME, THE WORKS THAT I DO
SHALL HE DO ALSO; AND GREATER WORKS
THAN THESE SHALL HE DO; BECAUSE I GO
UNTO MY FATHER."**

Listen to me very carefully now, Jesus is not
depending on our ability to do the Works He did. He
already said that He was doing His Father's Works,
God's Works, and He knows that - He is confident that
His Father's ability in us will do the same thing it did in
Him - it will break every yoke of bondage, and ... It Will
Set Every Captive Free including you and your loved
ones!

JESUS PUT GOD FIRST!

Do you remember how Jesus fulfilled His Ministry?
He grew up! Since He grew up, there is only one way
for us to be conformed to the image of the Lord Jesus
Christ.
We have to grow up!

Jesus grew up by reading and studying and doing God's Word. You will grow up by doing the same things. In Luke 2:46 He was both asking and answering questions. It is not hard to ask questions, but to answer them with God's Word, you have to study. God does not open up the top of your head like a lid and put the knowledge of His Word in you - you have to read, and you have to study. You must meditate on His Word and you must be a doer! - Not just a hearer only. Those were His Instructions to Joshua in Joshua 1:8, and those are still His Instructions to His People today.

You must put something in first if you want to get anything out!

Jesus put God First! He said in John 5:30,

"...I SEEK NOT MY OWN WILL, BUT THE WILL OF THE FATHER WHO SENT ME."

God's will was more important than His own will. He said,

"I do not do anything, and I do not say anything, that my Father does not tell me to do or say."

He committed His Will, His Mind, His Tongue, and His Life totally to His Father. The Lord did not depend on His own ability or on His own thought process; He did not depend on how He felt to accomplish what the Father sent Him to do. He depended upon His Father's Ability in Him.

Let's look at the account of Jesus' baptism.

Matthew 3:16 and 17, Mark 1:9-11, and Luke 3:21-22, all record this event. Let's read this account in Luke 3:21-22:

"NOW WHEN ALL THE PEOPLE WERE BAPTIZED, IT CAME TO PASS, THAT JESUS ALSO BEING BAPTIZED, AND PRAYING, THE HEAVEN WAS OPENED. AND THE HOLY GHOST DESCENDED IN A BODILY SHAPE LIKE A DOVE UPON HIM, AND A VOICE CAME FROM HEAVEN, WHICH SAID, 'THOU ART MY BELOVED SON; IN THEE I AM WELL PLEASED.' "

Have you ever wondered why the Lord spoke to Jesus and told Him, "He was His Beloved Son in whom He was well pleased," at this particular time? What had Jesus done up to now? He had not:

Walked on the water; He hadn't healed the sick; He hadn't fed the multitudes; He hadn't stilled the storm; He hadn't raised the dead! He hadn't preached the Gospel.

In fact, He had not proclaimed the Acceptable Year of the Lord, or performed any miracle or worked any mighty work. The only thing He had done was to grow up. But when God looked at His heart, He knew His Son was ready to meet every challenge of the devil! He knew He was adequately prepared to reconcile the world back to His Father, because when God looked at Jesus He saw a total reflection of Himself, and He said,

"THOU ART MY BELOVED SON; IN THEE I AM WELL PLEASED."

God was pleased with Jesus because He had grown up. By putting God's Will before His own Will, He became the express Image of what He and His Father planned for Him to become. Praise God! Do you think that since it worked for our example, that it might work for us? If we put God's Will before our will: if we only do and say what the Father tells us to do and to say - that we might just possibly become the person God plans for us to be. Of course we will!

That is why the Bible was written - for our instruction; to teach us, to show us how to live. It is "profitable" Timothy said in 2 Timothy 3:16. Could you use a profitable experience in your life? Could you use some profit?

> *Would you like for your Heavenly Father to speak to you and say, "This is my beloved son, or this is my beloved daughter, in whom I am well pleased."*

If you do, you will have to do what Jesus did - you will have to grow up! When you grow up, when you stop acting like a child, and thinking like a child, you will put God's Will before your own will, and you will get on about His business.

CONFORMED!

God has a tremendous plan for Believers! His plan is for every Believer to be conformed to the image of His Son. As hard as that is to believe in the natural, the Potter's plan for His clay is that you and I grow up to maturity, and that we become conformed to the image

of His Son. Since that is His plan, let's look at the one
we are to become conformed to:

**"IN THE BEGINNING WAS THE WORD, AND
THE WORD WAS WITH GOD, AND THE WORD
WAS GOD."**

**"HE WAS IN THE BEGINNING WITH GOD..."
John 1:2**

**"AND THE WORD BECAME FLESH, AND
DWELT AMONG US.." John 1:14**

Do you recognize why God was pleased with Jesus
before He had done anything except grow up?
     It was because the Word became flesh in Him. He
was the Word of God in the flesh.
     Do you know how you will become conformed to
His image? It is when the Word of God becomes flesh
in you. When God's Word becomes your word.
     Peter talked to us about that in 1 Peter 4:11,

**"IF ANY MAN SPEAK, LET HIM SPEAK AS THE
ORACLES OF GOD; ..."**

What does this Scripture mean? It means, "say
what God says."   Peter is telling us, "When you talk,
and I know you are going to talk, speak God's Words!"
     That is what Jesus did. He spoke His Father's
Words, and He is your example - your goal is to be like
Him! If God's Word is going to become flesh in your
life, you have to know what He said so you can speak
His Words instead of your words, won't you? Well, of
course you will.

The Bible is full of instructions like this. God told Joshua how to be prosperous and successful in life. He told Joshua how to take the Promised Land, and then He told him how to dwell in it. Isn't that what all of us want to do, to live in our Promised Land, in God's Land of Milk and Honey? In Joshua 1:8, God said,

"THIS BOOK OF THE LAW SHALL NOT DEPART OUT OF THY MOUTH; BUT THOU SHALT MEDITATE THEREIN DAY AND NIGHT. THAT THOU MAYEST OBSERVE TO DO ACCORDING TO ALL THAT IS WRITTEN THEREIN: FOR THEN THOU SHALT MAKE THY WAY PROSPEROUS, AND THEN THOU SHALT HAVE GOOD SUCCESS."

Are you interested in these things? Are you interested in God's success and prosperity in every area of your life? Did you notice who had to do the doing? Joshua did! God was not going to do for him, Gabriel was not going to do for him, and Moses had already gone to be with the Lord.

Joshua was going to have to do the doing for himself. - And so will you! But God provided the way, He gave him the method! Joshua was to speak God's Word! He was to meditate on the Word of God! And he was to be careful to do ALL that was written therein! Then and only then would Joshua have the right, and the authority, and the power to make his way prosperous, and to have good success.

You know that it is worth some doing on your part, some digging and some training, if you can get into the Land God has promised you in His Word. Of course it is! But to get there, you will have to be a doer of the Word and not a hearer only.

The only one who can get you into your Promised Land or keep you out of it, is you! You are the only one who can do the doing in your life. Read Joshua 1:1-9 and pay particular attention to Verse 8 that we read together above. The Bible teaches us that when Joshua followed God's instructions, He had God's Power and Authority in his life to do whatever he needed to do!

The First Psalm sets forth the same Biblical Principles. Let me share Verses 1-3 with you:

"HOW BLESSED IS THE MAN WHO DOES NOT WALK IN THE COUNSEL OF THE WICKED, NOR STAND IN THE PATH OF SINNERS, NOR SIT IN THE SEAT OF SCOFFERS!

BUT HIS DELIGHT IS IN THE LAW OF THE LORD, AND IN HIS LAW HE MEDITATES DAY AND NIGHT.

AND HE WILL BE LIKE A TREE FIRMLY PLANTED BY STREAMS OF WATER, WHICH YIELDS ITS FRUIT IN ITS SEASON, AND ITS LEAF DOES NOT WITHER; AND IN WHATEVER HE DOES, HE PROSPERS."

In whatever he does, he prospers! God wants us to prosper in life! God's plan is for us to study, to meditate, and then to do His Word! God has written His Book for us; He has recorded His plan. Now it is up to us to follow His instructions so we can be all the Lord designed us to be.

We can let God's Word become Flesh in our lives if we so choose! It is our choice.

We can do His Will, or we can insist on doing our own thing. It is entirely up to us. It is His Will or our will. And the only way we can know His Will is to read His Word.

God will not rule in our kingdom; He only rules in His Kingdom. If we always insist on being the King in our kingdom instead of being obedient to His Word, then He is not ruling in us, and we cannot dwell in the Kingdom of God. It is our choice. We can allow God to take His throne in our life, or we can continue to rule ourselves.

Two kings cannot rule the same kingdom at the same time.

CHAPTER FIFTEEN
MADE IN HIS IMAGE

Let's look at Genesis 1:26 again:

"AND GOD SAID, LET US MAKE MAN IN OUR IMAGE, AFTER OUR LIKENESS..."

Verse 27 says God did just that. So, since you are made in the image of God, what part of you looks like God? Is it your nose? Your eyes? Your smile? Your beautiful face?

When you think about it, you know that the part of you that is made in His image is your inner man - your spirit! It is Christ in you who is your hope of Glory! The Lord comes to reside in you when you receive Him as your personal Savior, and you are indwelt by the Lord! (Remember - it is not how you look on the outside that gets the job done, it is how you feel inside.)

Think with me now - Since God made you in His image, have you ever wondered how the devil knows that it is you he is messing around with instead of God? I mean when he comes prowling around your house, like Peter said in 1 Peter 5:8,

"...YOUR ADVERSARY, THE DEVIL, PROWLS AROUND LIKE A ROARING LION, SEEKING SOMEONE TO DEVOUR."

Has he ever prowled around in your life, shaking your windows and rattling your doors? He will you know. And when he comes he will try to bring sickness, poverty, death, discouragement and doom with him to call on you if you will allow him.

May I ask you that question again, how does the devil know it is you he is messing around with instead of God? You know the Bible says God made you in His image and in His likeness. Do you think the devil could do to God what he is doing to you?

Well, do you know how the devil knows who is who in You? How he knows it is you he is messing around with instead of God? It is by the way you act and by the way you react to the circumstances he puts in your life. It is by what you do with the cards he deals you in life - you have to remember that 2 Corinthians 4:4 calls him the god of this world, so he does have some power in this world.

The devil is not your God, but he can bring some detrimental circumstances in your life. Remember he had Paul and Silas thrown in Jail at Philippi.

How do you deal with him then - how do you confuse the familiar spirits operating in your life? How do you make familiar spirits, unfamiliar?

You can confuse the familiar spirits operating in your life by reacting to every situation like God's Word instructs you to. By looking at the Word instead of being overcome by the circumstances that you find yourself temporarily bogged down in, or surrounded by.

Let me show you an example in Isaiah 11:1-2:

"AND THERE SHALL COME FORTH A ROD OUT OF THE STEM OF JESSE, AND A BRANCH SHALL GROW OUT OF HIS ROOTS.

AND THE SPIRIT OF THE LORD SHALL REST UPON HIM, THE SPIRIT OF WISDOM AND UNDERSTANDING, THE SPIRIT OF COUNSEL AND MIGHT, THE SPIRIT OF KNOWLEDGE AND OF THE FEAR OF THE LORD;"

Isaiah, prophesying about the Lord Jesus Christ said He would have the seven spirits of God. We know this prophesy came to pass, we know Jesus had the seven spirits of God, because Revelation 3:1 says:

"AND TO THE ANGEL OF THE CHURCH IN SARDIS WRITE; HE WHO HAS THE SEVEN SPIRITS OF GOD SAYS THIS..."

Revelation 5:5-6 further documents this fact,

"Christ, the lion that is from the tribe of Judah has the seven spirits of God" (My paraphrase).

Christ had the Seven Spirits of God. You can see by looking at these Scriptures that Isaiah's prophecy in 11:1-2 was fulfilled. Now let's see how and where the rest of His prophecy was fulfilled. In Isaiah 11:3 He said,

"AND HE (CHRIST) WILL DELIGHT IN THE FEAR OF THE LORD, AND HE WILL NOT JUDGE BY WHAT HIS EYES SEE, NOR MAKE A DECISION BY WHAT HIS EARS HEAR."

Christ, the One who has the Seven Spirits of God, the Holy one of Israel, will not judge by what His eyes see, nor make a decision by what His ears hear. Is that too heavy for you? Does this sound familiar to you at all, this teaching on faith in the Old Testament?

The Lord Jesus Christ did not depend on His sense nature when what His senses told Him contradicted the Word of God. He depended entirely upon His Father.

"Whoa! Wait a minute, brother!" I can almost hear some of you saying. "I can't do that. "I know that Isaiah 53:5 says 'By His Stripes we are healed', but when my senses tell me I hurt, or that I do not feel good - Common sense tells me that I am sick. And everyone has to be sick sometime.

I know the Bible says, 'Give and it shall be given unto you,' but common sense tells me that $1.00 goes a lot farther than a tithed 90 Cents.

That is one of the devil's favorite phrases. Common sense tells you that what the Bible tells you is not true!

"Common sense tells me this and common sense tells me that..."

Listen to me carefully now, you need to realize that when common sense contradicts the Word of God, that it is exactly what it is called ... common.

It is the kind of sense that everyone has, saint, as well as the sinner!

In fact, some sinners seem to have more common sense than some Christians.

Why do you think it is called common? Because, it is common to everyone! And when you continue to walk by your sense nature, when your sense nature contradicts God's Word, you will spend most of your life walking on coals. And I guarantee you they will be hot ones, because the guy with the pitchfork, and the long pointed tail will find you out - he will find out what makes you tick; he will find out that he can control you with circumstances. And when he does, he will bring that bunch of demons that Believers all over the world have cast out of their lives, and they will all come over to your house for a cookout. And the first thing they will do, is build a roaring fire to make sure that the coals are nice and hot, and then they will have you walking on their bed of coals and dancing to their tune for the rest of your life.

In fact, I think some of you have been dancing to the devil's tune for so long now that you are beginning to do special requests for him. Every time he zings you with a pain, or with a sharp look, or with an unexpected bill, or with a little rejection, you do exactly what he wants you to do. You invite the Three Stooges right back into your life again.

Do you want to listen to a recording that the devil or some of his imps might have made around the Church? Or around your dinner table?

"I gave in the offering, so I just don't know why I am broke. Why don't I have plenty of money?"

"I thought I was healed, but now I am hurting again, so I must still be sick."

"They told me God's Word worked, but just look at my life since I began going to Church."

"Why am I unhappy?   Why am I lonely?   Why doesn't my spouse treat me better? Why...?"

You might as well sweep off your front porch - and put out the welcome mat for Doubt, Despair, and Doom.   You can start baking them a cake because those guys will join you momentarily.   The Three Stooges never turn an invitation down! And when you begin to deny the validity of God's Word, you give them the special invitation they have been waiting for to move in with you.

2 Corinthians 5:7 proclaims,

"...FOR WE WALK BY FAITH, NOT BY SIGHT."

If you never learn to walk by faith in the Word of God, if you always walk by sight - that means by your sense nature - you will never have a choice on what you do in this life.   The devil will make all the choices for you because you have turned your decision making rights over to him, and he will start up his Pow Wow in you right away.

Listen, can you hear the drums?   Dum-dum -dum-dumb-dumb-dumb-dumb!   He always plays the same tune.   Does it have a familiar beat?   Have you danced to that tune a time or two before?

IS ALL THIS REALLY TRUE?

Is all this really true? Did Jesus ever have to do that? Did he ever have to refuse to judge by what His eyes saw, and by what His ears heard? Did He ever have to walk by faith, and not by sight? Sure He did - all through the Bible. Let me give you one example.

The account of Lazarus is recorded in John 11. Lazarus' sisters sent a message to Jesus in John 11:3 saying,

"LORD, BEHOLD, HE WHOM YOU LOVE IS SICK."

I want you to note Jesus' reaction to the bad news. He did not cry or whimper, or wring His hands! He said in John 11:4,

"...THIS SICKNESS IS NOT UNTO DEATH, BUT FOR THE GLORY OF GOD, THAT THE SON OF GOD MAY BE GLORIFIED BY IT."

Do you know Jesus loved Lazarus? Sure He did; He felt about Lazarus the same way you feel about your loved ones. Jesus has feelings. The message Mary and Martha sent was, "Lord, the one you love is sick!" Think with me now, when the devil tried to send Jesus a message of Doubt, Despair, and Doom, about His loved ones, He was not going to have any - He did not accept the message Satan sent to Him. He responded with words of faith. He said,

"THIS SICKNESS IS NOT UNTO DEATH, BUT FOR THE GLORY OF GOD..."!

Jesus did not say Lazarus was not sick. He did not deny sickness. He declared that the devil was not going to get any glory out of His life, or out of the lives of His loved ones.

Do you think this was what He was teaching us in Mark 11:23 and 24 when He said,

"FOR VERILY I SAY UNTO YOU, THAT WHOSOEVER SHALL SAY UNTO THIS MOUNTAIN, BE THOU REMOVED, AND BE THOU CAST INTO THE SEA; AND SHALL NOT DOUBT IN HIS HEART, BUT SHALL BELIEVE THAT THOSE THINGS WHICH HE SAITH SHALL COME TO PASS; HE SHALL HAVE WHATSOEVER HE SAITH."

"THEREFORE I SAY UNTO YOU, WHAT THINGS SOEVER YE DESIRE, WHEN YE PRAY, BELIEVE THAT YE RECEIVE THEM, AND YE SHALL HAVE THEM."

Jesus had already done some praying and some saying about His loved ones, and He was not going to throw away His confidence in His Father just because He had received an evil report.

You can do that, you know! You can hold fast your confidence!

You can meet every evil report with a positive response from the Word of God! The devil delights in sending you reports, and none of them are singing telegrams telling you everything is going to be all right, are they? Of course, they are not! He is constantly bringing you an evil report! Jesus said in John 10:10,

"THE THIEF COMES ONLY TO STEAL, AND TO KILL, AND TO DESTROY..."

The devil has come to destroy you, but before he can do that, he has to steal the validity of God's Word away from you. The devil cannot kill you or destroy you until he steals God's promise in His Word from you. The devil works the same way all the time - He will send you a report

of sickness, or poverty, or strife, or anxiousness, or inadequacy, or want, or lack ...or some other dumb thing.

Jesus said he is a thief. What kind of message do you think the thief is going to send to you? It would seem that after he has stolen from you for awhile, that you would begin to treat him like the thief that he is, and start guarding your mind and your heart against him.

Jesus did!

When the thief stole Lazarus' health, he immediately sent word to Jesus that the one He loved was sick. Do you realize that he was trying to get Jesus to make a mistake! He was trying to get Him to panic! - To walk by His senses.

But thank God, Jesus was not going to play the devil's game. He came to do His Father's Will, not to dance to the devil's tune! Jesus immediately began to make some faith declarations.

Our Example began to say good! You ought to try doing that in your life sometime. Let me assure you, you will be pleased with the results.

As you continue reading this account, you'll see in Verse 14 that Jesus said,

"LAZARUS IS DEAD."

Sometime between Verse 4 when Jesus said **"THIS SICKNESS IS NOT UNTO DEATH,.."** and Verse 14, Lazarus died. What would that do to your faith? If you were the one who said, "This sickness is not unto death," and then the one about whom you had made these faith declarations died - would that discourage you a little? Would you quit? Would you get mad at God and have a temper tantrum? Would you say,

"Where are you God? Why didn't my confession work? I said all the right things! Why did you let this terrible thing happen to me?"

Aren't you glad Jesus did not react this way? - Jesus held fast His confession. He had prayed about Lazarus - He had taken His stand on God's Word, and common sense combined with all the negative circumstantial evidence in the world and in hell put together was not going to keep Him from receiving what God's Word promised.

Jesus went on to Bethany and when He got there, do you know what His ears heard and what His eyes saw?

His ears heard the weeping and wailing of Martha and Mary and of all the Jews who had come to watch them mourn. His ears heard Martha cry, "BUT LORD, HE STINKETH!" His eyes saw the tears, and they saw the stone that was rolled up to the tomb where Lazarus was buried.

But Jesus was not convinced by what His eyes saw and by what His ears heard, when what His eyes saw and what His ears heard contradicted The Word of God.

In Verse 41 John records,

"...JESUS RAISED HIS EYES, AND SAID,'FATHER, I THANK THEE THAT THOU HEARDEST ME.' 'AND I KNEW THAT THOU HEAREST ME ALWAYS; BUT BECAUSE OF THE PEOPLE STANDING AROUND I SAID IT, THAT THEY MAY BELIEVE THAT THOU DIDST SEND ME.'

AND WHEN HE HAD SAID THESE THINGS, HE CRIED OUT WITH A LOUD VOICE, 'LAZARUS, COME FORTH.' "

And guess who came out of the grave? Why Lazarus did! Of course!

The man who had been dead for four days came walking out of the grave!

Jesus only said what His Father told Him to say, so His Father must have told him to tell Lazarus to come out of that impossible situation called the grave. Jesus knew that God's Word was settled in Heaven forever (Psalm 119:89), and since God's Word was settled in Him; He did what God told Him to do!

Do you think God's Word will ever be settled in You? Is it possible for God's Word to be settled in you? Let me tell you how you will know. When God's Word is settled in you, God's Word will be the final authority in your life in every situation.

And then - God will use His Word in you to call you out of the impossible situations the devil has been trying to put you in!

CHAPTER SIXTEEN

WHAT DOES ALL THIS HAVE TO DO WITH YOU?

What does all this have to do with you? How do these Scriptures relate to you and to your life? How will the account of Lazarus help you in your everyday living?

Well, the devil thought he had trapped Jesus. He had made one of His best friends sick, and then he killed him. Lazarus was dead and buried in the grave! But Jesus whom God anointed with the Holy Ghost and with Power, broke the bondage of death in Lazarus' life. What a tremendous victory!

Think about how Jesus acted. Can you imagine the confusion Jesus caused in hell? Pandemonium must have broken loose in hell when Lazarus rose and marched triumphantly out of the grave!

The messengers between Bethany and the devil's command post were probably exhausted as they dashed back and forth carrying a blow-by-blow description of what Jesus was saying and doing to the devil.

Maybe they thought Jesus had given up when He wept in John 11:35. Remember that Scripture? "JESUS WEPT." Maybe they started a pep rally in hell cheering the devil because they thought he had won. Their cheers may have sounded something like your cheers at your high school pep rally. **Remember them?** Your cheers may have sounded something like this,

> *"Two - four - six - eight - Who do we appreciate?" Then you would shout, "Eagles! Bulldogs! Chiefs! Rams!" Or whatever the name of your team was.*

At the devil's pep rally **his** followers may have been shouting,

> *"Yipptie Dipptie Doooo - Just look at all the bad stuff the devil can do!" And*

> *"Ricktie Racktie Russ, who are we gonna cuss!"*

> *Then they would begin to shout and cheer for the devil!"*

I don't know how they cheer in hell. (I do know there is no cheer down there, just a bunch of misery and gloom.) I don't know how they shout and carry on in the pit, but I am sure that they don't sing the Doxology,

> *"Praise God from whom all blessings flow."*

In any event, they were dumbfounded, and confusion must have reigned when Jesus shouted,

> *"Lazarus, come forth!" And Lazarus came forth! He did what Jesus told him to do.*

The Lord Jesus Christ took dominion over death! He was doing what He had been born to do, "to take dominion."

Would you like to do that? Would you like to create a little confusion among the spirits who have been creating confusion and bringing evil into your life?

Let me tell you how you can do it. You can make that bunch who have been punching you around - punch the pandemonium button! - if you will react to every situation exactly like God's Word instructs you. If you will let God's Word become flesh in your flesh!

Let's take a hypothetical situation. The devil has a headquarters somewhere - Here on the earth or some where below the earth. And in his headquarters is the control center where he wages spiritual warfare against us. This is where he gives directions to his demons and angels and other spirits. You know he is not present everywhere - he does not have that power. The devil can only be at one specific place at a time. He is a created being, and he cannot occupy more than one space at one time. Most of the time, the space he is occupying is in his headquarters - where he is busy checking on demon activity and plotting and scheming against us.

Now I want to take you, in this hypothetical situation, to the Command Post where the Familiar Spirits, who are assigned to you, are making a progress report to their master, the devil.

They do have a reporting system, and the devil is a taskmaster!

Do you know that? He is a slave driver, and all those who serve him are slaves, the spirits as well as the humans. Slaves always get treated like slaves by the devil. Have you ever noticed how the devil treats those who are under his power? Look at the drug addicts, or the alcoholics, or the thieves, or the prostitutes, or the liars. Take a look at the cults, and see the things they do. Why, some of them even have to dress in peculiar clothing, some have to shave their heads, some have to beg for money, and all of them have to turn their minds and their privacy over to their leaders.

The devil is a taskmaster! The devil is a slave driver, because he deals with slaves.

The spiritual beings who serve him have even less freedom than the humans who serve him. They are slaves, too, and the reporting-in process is not pleasant. It is full of fear and anxiety and dread.

Spirits possess their own characteristics! What do I mean by that? Well, poverty spirits are broke, they are poverty stricken; fear spirits are fearful (have you ever felt that spirit in someone); strife spirits are full of strife; homosexual spirits are full of homosexual acts! The devil's headquarters is chock full of pandemonium and fear and strife all the time because that is home for those spirits, and it is not home sweet home either. Their home is hell, literally and figuratively!

Reporting in time is especially stressful and full of strife for this bunch, because they are forced to give an account on how they are doing with you, and the Bible says that where strife is, every evil thing is present. Every evil thing is present in hell - it is terrible! Maybe the eternal fire is raging, and the tar pits are bubbling - maybe there are cries of fear and anguish. It is hot and horrible and

everyone is forced to stand rigidly at attention!

waiting for the devil to call on them. Then he points to one of them, and the reporting process begins:

The poverty spirit is first! This spirit is almost always first because it has managed to convince many people in the Church that they have to be poor, broke, and hungry to serve God. Then when the devil says, "Report!" this spirit begins to squirm.

"I am doing my best," he whines, "but God's Word is becoming flesh in my human, and every time I try to put my Poverty Spirit on him, he begins to quote Philippians 4:14-19 to me. My human says,

'I am giving unto the Gospel and my God is supplying all my needs according to His riches in glory by Christ Jesus!'

The poverty spirit continues, 'I cannot keep him broke any more since he found out that when he gives, God causes good to be given unto him.' "

Now it is the sick spirit's turn! The devil chuckles with glee when the sick spirit comes up because he has done his number about sickness on the Church for years. He has always been able to persuade a bunch of Christians that it is God's Will for them to be sick - that God is teaching them some profound Spiritual lesson while He is making them miserable.

But this time the sick spirit begins to grovel and cry, "It has always worked before, but now something is different. Every time I try to make my human sick, he just begins to sing Isaiah 53:5 to me. Oh! I hate that song!

Because when he believes what he sings, I have lost my power. My human just smiles and sings,

'He was wounded for my transgressions, He was bruised for my iniquities, the chastisement of my peace was upon Him, and by His stripes I am healed.'

The sick spirit complains, 'I am just not effective any more, I cannot make him sick because he refuses to accept the sickness I am trying to give him.'"

Now it is the anxious spirit's turn. It is time for one of the devil's favorite spirits to report, and I can almost see the devil gloating as this quartet of worry, anxiety, fear, and gloom slink up to the microphones. But this time instead of harmonizing together they are murmuring and complaining.

"It does not work any more," they say anxiously, "something has happened to the humans we have been harassing. They will not listen to our tune any more, when we try to get them to *worry, or to get uptight, or to be fearful, they just say,*

'The Holy Ghost told us in Philippians 4:6 and 7 that we do not have to be anxious about anything, but in every thing with prayer and supplication, with thanksgiving, we can make our specific requests known unto God, and the peace of God which passes all comprehension belongs to us.'

Then almost in despair they cry out to the devil,

'They are beginning to sound like Jesus of Nazareth, The Holy One of Israel - what is Happening! Has something gone wrong? Is it the time? Is your plan working? Have we failed? Have we been deceived?'"

Then the unworthy spirit shows up. The spirit who has kept lots of folks in bondage, the one who usually struts in gloating, is now telling a much different story.

"When I whisper my message of 'You are not big enough, you are not pretty enough, you are not strong enough, you are not worthy,' to my humans, they just smile and say:

'We are not depending on our own worthiness, because the Bible says that we are in right standing with God through Christ Jesus! We do not have to depend on how we feel inside, or *on how we look on the outside, because we are depending on God's ability in us to get the job done!'"*

Listen to me now, you can create mass confusion in the spirit world! You can defeat the spirits that the devil has assigned to your case when you learn to react to every situation exactly as God's Word instructs you to react. You can let the Word become flesh in your life.

And when you do, the first thing you know you will have those old Familiar Spirits who have messed up your life begging for a transfer. They will want to go to a rest home so they can relax a little before they all have a nervous breakdown. Hallelujah! Wouldn't you like to make them nervous and uneasy and anxious for a change?

Don't you think it is about time you begin to act like the creature you were created to be? Read Genesis 1:26 again - the Bible really says that God created you in His own image, and in His likeness. He created you to take dominion over all the Works of His Hands.

God did not create you to be a poverty stricken, sickly, worry laden, unhappy, unworthy, inadequate new creature!

You are made in His Image and none of those things are in the image of God, are they? Of course not, He made you to be a winner, and if you will let His Word reign in you, you can reign in life through Christ Jesus. You will be a winner every time, all the time. In fact, the Holy Spirit told us in Romans 5:17,

that we are to reign in life through Christ Jesus.

That is your new image in Christ! A reigning in life image!

Well, that is what God created you for - to reign, and to rule, and to take dominion over all the Works of His Hands, including the devil and that bunch of familiar spirits who have been trying to reign over you.

GOD'S PLAN FOR YOU!

You can confuse the Familiar Spirits who are assigned to you if you will meet every situation, every problem, every challenge the devil hurls at you with the Word of God.

You will always defeat the devil's challenges in your life - when you say just what the Father said, when you become an oracle of God, when you let the Word become flesh in you.

That is what Jesus did. He confused the devil and all of his helpers! They did not know what to do with Him. They could not handle Jesus, and they can not handle you! Jesus is your example. Romans 8:29 says it is God's Will that you become like His Son, and His Son did not judge by what His eyes saw, or by what His ears heard. He did not rely on His senses when His senses contradicted God's Word. He depended on His Father's Word!

"I ONLY DO WHAT I SEE MY FATHER DOING."
"I ONLY SAY WHAT MY FATHER TELLS ME TO SAY."

"I DID NOT COME TO SEEK MY OWN WILL, BUT TO SEEK THE WILL OF MY FATHER IN HEAVEN."

You can do that! The Word of God can become flesh in your life. God's tremendous, wonderful, exhilarating, beautiful plan for you, is that you become conformed to the image of His Son.

You can have your druthers! You do not have to be inadequate, or unworthy, or lonely, or sick, or broke, or poverty stricken. You do not have to be defeated in any area of your life.

You can have your druthers when you learn God's Word. When you meditate on His Word - When you speak His Word, and when you become a doer of His Word - not just a hearer only.

You can make that bunch of Familiar Spirits who have taken such delight in harassing you and trying to make your life miserable, **unfamiliar!** You can create havoc with the spirits who are assigned to your case, when you learn to rely upon God's Word in every circumstance.

Come on! Get into God's Word and let His plan work in you! You can become conformed to the Image of His Son. You can do it because that is God's Will for your life. Do not seek your own will, Beloved, seek His!

You are a winner because Jesus is a winner!
You are living in Him and He is living in you!

1 John 4:4 declares triumphantly,

"...GREATER IS HE WHO IS IN YOU, THAN HE WHO IS IN THE WORLD!..."

That should be your daily confession. Shout it from your roof top for all the world to hear - startle every demon between your house and hell with your declaration of who and what you are in Christ! You are who you are, you have authority over them, because of whose you are!

FINAL WORDS

Listen to me carefully, you know now that what you do with your life is up to you. You are responsible for you. Jesus told us in John 8:31 and 32,

"...IF YOU ABIDE IN MY WORD, THEN YOU ARE TRULY DISCIPLES OF MINE; AND YOU SHALL KNOW THE TRUTH, AND THE TRUTH SHALL MAKE YOU FREE."

The only question now is - Do you really want to be free?

If you do, you will abide in His Word - and when you abide in His Word - you shall know the Truth, and the truth of His Word will set you free! Thank God for His freedom Provisions in Christ! One of the best things of all about His freedom Provisions is that all of them - every single one of them - belong to you!

You have the right in Christ to be free from Sin -

To be free from Inadequacy -

To be free from Loneliness -
To be free from Poverty -
To be free from Sickness -
To be free from Lack or Want of any kind.

The Holy Spirit told us in Galatians 5:1,

"IT WAS FOR FREEDOM THAT CHRIST SET US FREE; THEREFORE KEEP STANDING FIRM AND DO NOT BE SUBJECT AGAIN TO A YOKE OF SLAVERY."

Be determined that you will not be subject to the devil's yoke of bondage in any area of your life ever again.

Enjoy your Freedom in Christ!

TEACHING BOOKS BY ROBERT SHACKELFORD

"FAMILIAR SPIRITS" $7.95

A Spiritual Warfare Manual that will teach you how you can use God's Word to defeat the spirits who are trying to make your life miserable. Over 50,000 copies in print.

"PROMISED LAND INSTRUCTIONS" $7.95

Does God have a promised land for you? If He does, how do you leave the wilderness and get into Canaan Land? Does it seem as if all of God's promises belong to almost everyone except you sometimes? Do you feel as if you are living on the wrong side of the Jordan River looking longingly at the Promised Land? This book is designed to teach you how to occupy and then live in the Promised Land God has for you.

"BENEFITS OF RIGHTEOUSNESS" $4.95

This book sets forth the difference in the "Righteousness" imputed at salvation, and the "Righteousness" that is to be practiced in your life. God has a standard of conduct for every Believer, and as we live by His standards, His blessings will abound in our lives.

YOU MAY ORDER FROM:
Bob Shackelford, P. O. Box 101,
Delaware, OH 43015

When ordering please add $1 for postage and handling for each book.

EILEEN SIMPSON is the author of the critically acclaimed *Poets in Their Youth, Reversals,* and *The Maze,* as well as many articles, short stories, and reviews. She is a practicing psychotherapist living in New York City.

ORPHANS
Real and Imaginary

EILEEN SIMPSON

A PLUME BOOK

NEW AMERICAN LIBRARY

NEW YORK AND SCARBOROUGH, ONTARIO

The author gratefully acknowledges permission to reprint from the following:

First Love and Other Shorts by Samuel Beckett. Copyright © 1974 by Samuel
Beckett. Reprinted by permission of Grove Press, Inc.

The Autobiography of Bertrand Russell by Bertrand Russell. Copyright © 1967 by
Bertrand Russell. Reprinted by permission of Allen & Unwin Publishers Ltd.

Collected Poems of Stevie Smith by Stevie Smith. Copyright © 1972 by Stevie
Smith. Reprinted by permission of New Directions Publishing Corporation.

Library of Congress Cataloging-in-Publication Data

Simpson, Eileen B.
  Orphans : real and imaginary.

  Bibliography: p.
  1. Simpson, Eileen B. 2. Orphans—United States—
Biography. 3. Orphans. 4. Orphans in literature.
I. Title.
[HV983.S55 1988]   362.7'9 [B]   88-1414
ISBN 0-452-26060-4 (pbk.)

Original hardcover designed by Irving Perkins Associates

First Plume Printing, July, 1988

1 2 3 4 5 6 7 8 9

PRINTED IN THE UNITED STATES OF AMERICA

FOR MARIE, MY COMPANION
IN THE WILDERNESS.

Contents

It is, or it is not, according to the nature of men, an advantage to be orphaned at an early age.

—DE QUINCEY

ORPHANS
Real and Imaginary